KU-325-391

A Guide to Angling Law

DISPOSED OF
BY LIBRARY
HOUSE OF LORDS

DISPOSED OF
BY LIBRARY
HOUSE OF LORDS

A Guide to Angling Law

by

Ronald Millichamp, F.I.F.M.

SHAW & SONS LTD
Shaway House,
Crayford, Kent.

Published in 1990 by Shaw & Sons Ltd.,
Crayford, Kent, DA1 4BZ.
Typeset by P & I Publications
Farnborough, GU14 7QY.
Printed by Bell & Bain Ltd.,
Glasgow, G46 7UQ.

A CIP catalogue record for this
book is available from the British Library.

ISBN 07219 12400

*No part of this publication may be reproduced
or transmitted in any form without the written
permission of the copyright holder and publisher,
application for which shall be made to the publisher.*

©
Shaw & Sons Ltd.
1990

FOREWORD

By
The Lord Moran K.C.M.G.
Chairman, Regional Fisheries Advisory Committee,
Welsh Region,
National Rivers Authority.

Those concerned with fisheries can just as easily become entangled in legal complexities as they can get a monofilment line in an inextricable muddle. Indeed, there is now a considerable body of legislation affecting fisheries and a consequent need for a clear and comprehensive guide, addressed to the layman, which can help anglers, fishery managers, riparian owners and others to find their way quickly through the provisions of fishery law as it affects them. This book answers that need.

The author, Ron Millichamp, is admirably qualified to produce it. He has had long and varied practical experience in controlling fisheries first as a Head Bailiff, and later as a Fisheries and Recreation Officer in different parts of the country. Both as a founder member and Fellow of the Institute of Fisheries Management and as a consultant on the training of bailiffs and wardens, he has had a wide experience of fishery law and its enforcement. He is also an active member of the Regional Fisheries Advisory Committee of the Welsh Region of the National Rivers Authority.

I recommend this book to all concerned with the fisheries in this country.

Moran
May 1990

ACKNOWLEDGEMENTS

I am particularly indebted to Bill Howarth who found the time and had the patience to comment on, and criticise the contents of this book. I must also thank colleagues on both sides of the Border for putting me right on many points – however, any errors that remain are entirely of my own making.

Finally, my thanks to Alan Sugar for his word processor which made the task of writing so much easier!

CONTENTS

Part Three - Appendices

INTRODUCTION

About this book

The law, in the form of Acts of Parliament (Statute Law) and the Common Law, is often inaccessible to the layman and, even if he manages to locate it, difficult to comprehend, as much of it is couched in language which it takes a lawyer to interpret!

As both the common and statute law is written using expressions and terminology that the layman may find difficult to comprehend, in writing this book I have attempted to overcome this problem by paraphrasing, where it seems expedient to do so, the relevant parts of the law in the hope that it will be more easily understood without losing sight of the original meaning.

Most of the fisheries legislation covers all forms of fishing including commercial fishing. Those sections which refer to angling form a very small part of the whole but are, nevertheless, of prime importance to the rod fisherman and, consequently, it is those parts of the Acts only which are dealt with in this book.

Much of the subject matter is dealt with in general terms as in practice circumstances alter cases – for this reason the reader should not accept the text as the final answer to a particular problem but rather as a guide to help prevent the law being broken by anglers and to assist fishery owners and tenants in protecting their rights.

For a deeper and more detailed appreciation of the legal interpretation of fishery law, and examples of the case law which affect it, the reader is referred to some of the recommended reading matter given in Appendix H.

If litigation is involved or envisaged professional advice should always be sought.

Definitions

As some of the terms and abbreviations used in the text and in the Acts may be unfamiliar, the following definitions will apply, when appropriate. Scottish definitions are different in many cases from those used in England and Wales and a separate list to meet this is included in Part Two, which deals with the law and practices in Scotland.

"1968 Act" means the Theft Act 1968.

"1974 Act" and "C.O.P.A." means the Control of Pollution Act 1974.

"1975 Act" means the Salmon and Freshwater Fisheries Act 1975.

"1984 Act" means the Police and Criminal Evidence Act 1984.

"1986 Act" means the Salmon Act 1986.

"1989 Act" means the Water Act 1989.

"The Authority" and "N.R.A." means the National Rivers Authority.

"S.F.C." means Sea Fisheries Committee.

"Byelaw" means a byelaw made under the various fishery Acts.

"Tidal water" means the waters around the coast and in estuaries up to the tidal limit.

"Salmon" means all fish of the salmon species and includes part of a salmon.

"Trout" means any fish of the salmon family commonly known as trout, including migratory trout and char, and also includes part of a trout.

"Migratory trout" (sea-trout) means trout which migrate to and from the sea. Due to their migratory habits these fish are often linked with salmon in byelaws.

"Freshwater fish" (coarse fish) means any fish living in freshwater but excluding salmon, trout, eels and fish which migrate to and from tidal waters.

"Eels" include elvers.

"Game fish" means salmon, trout and char.

"Owner" includes any person who is entitled to receive rents from a fishery.

"Riparian owner" means the person owning the land adjoining a fishery.

"Tenant" in relation to a fishery includes any person for the time being in actual possession of the fishery.

"Angling" means fishing by means of a rod and line.

"Angler" means a person fishing by means of a rod and line.

The above will apply unless the context requires otherwise when the change is emphasised in the text, e.g. if rainbow trout are not included in part of the 1975 Act, the term "other than rainbow trout" will be used.

Part 1

ENGLAND AND WALES

Chapter 1

FISHERIES ADMINISTRATION

1.1 Overall responsibility

The overall responsibility for fisheries lies with the Minister of Agriculture, Fisheries and Food and, in the case of Wales, the Secretary of State for Wales. This responsibility is defined and embodied in the various Acts of Parliament and encompasses salmon, trout, freshwater and sea fisheries.

The responsibility is delegated, in part, to the bodies created under the various Acts to enforce their provisions – the National Rivers Authority (N.R.A.) through its ten regional units, in the case of salmon, trout and freshwater fish, and sea fisheries committees (S.F.C.) in the case of sea fish. However, the Minister or the Secretary of State still has the responsibility of approving any byelaws or orders which the Authority or committees may wish to introduce.

The Theft Act 1968, which has a partial (but important) application to fisheries, empowers the public to act against persons fishing unlawfully on private fisheries.

It is the responsibility of an owner or tenant to enforce the common law as it applies to or affects his rights of fishery ownership or tenancy. This is usually through the civil, not the criminal, courts.

1.2 The evolution and role of the N.R.A.

Prior to 1948, fisheries administration was in the hands of conservancy boards, each one being responsible for a single river system or group of adjoining systems; pollution control was in the hands of the local authorities, but as they were probably the biggest pollutors not a lot was done to bring it under control; and land drainage was the responsibility of local drainage boards who shared with the conservancy boards the common bond of lack of resources. The three functions operated independently and often in opposition to each other.

Under the River Board Act 1948 these functions were brought together under 28 new organisations, the river boards, and resulted in the demise of the bodies previously responsible for them. The river boards were for the first time able to integrate the various facets of river basin management and, aided by the Rivers (Prevention of Pollution) Acts 1951 and 1961, to control the discharge of effluents, monitor river pollution effectively and act against pollutors.

In 1963 the Water Resources Act reconstructed the boards into river authorities with the same role but with the added responsibility of managing the water resources within their areas. Their powers were strengthened by later legislation which gave greater control over discharges that had previously been exempt, including those into tidal waters. It was during this period that the clean-up of the polluted rivers of the country, such as the Tyne, the Thames and many of the rivers in industrial South Wales, reached a peak leading to the return of salmon, sea trout and many species of freshwater fish which had forsaken them decades before.

The Water Act 1973 again reorganised the industry. This time it amalgamated the river authorities into 10 new bodies – the water authorities – and gave them the added responsibility for water supply and sewage disposal. Each of the new authorities was much bigger than any of the individual river authorities they replaced and now had the resources to do many things which had previously not been possible. Many people, however, saw this as a retrograde step, in particular the dual responsibility for sewage disposal and pollution control which was regarded as a conflict of interests, and a reversion to the position prior to 1948.

This situation was rectified by yet more legislation and another reorganisation under the Water Act 1989. The service functions of water supply and sewage disposal became the responsibility of private companies while the regulatory and environmental functions, including fisheries became the responsibility of a new body, the National Rivers Authority, which provides among other things independent monitoring and control over the activities of the private companies and creates a similar situation to that which existed under the 1963 Act.

The stages which have led to the formation of the National Rivers Authority since 1948 are shown diagrammatically in Figure 1.

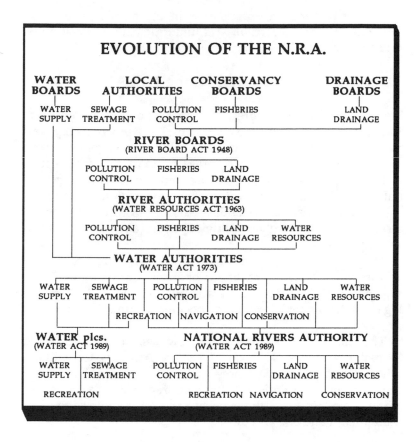

Figure 1

1.3 Reorganisation and administration

Fortunately the fishery powers and responsibilities of each succeeding body were contained in the Salmon and Freshwater Fisheries Act 1923 and superseding Acts in 1972, 1975, 1986 and 1989, whose provisions were taken over by each new body as it was formed so that there was a relatively smooth transition as far as this function was concerned. The main change each time was in managerial policy, priorities and staff organisation, but there were no significant changes in the enforcement of the law.

With each reorganisation the resources available for fisheries grew and the service it was able to offer improved. However, recent restrictions on expenditure in the public sector have prevented further expansion and, unfortunately in some cases, caused it to retract.

1.4 Fishery organization in the N.R.A.

The N.R.A. operates at present from its London headquarters through its 10 regional units. Each unit has its own fishery staff including fishery officers and water bailiffs whose role is geared to deal with the type of fishery prevalent in its area. Irrespective of the region certain basic tasks are common to all and include enforcement of fishery legislation, fish propagation, stocking etc.

In addition there are scientists who carry out environmental monitoring which involves biological, chemical, hydrological and fishery surveys.

This is all backed up by an administration which may be entirely within the fisheries department or form part of the N.R.A's. regional administration. Such would include secretarial services, legal advice and prosecutions, personnel administration and finance.

The link between anglers, fishery owners, etc. and the N.R.A. is established through Regional Fishery Advisory Committees whose members include representatives of different bodies and organisations. Its role is to advise the regional unit on fishery matters making use of the expertise and local knowledge of its individual members.

1.5 N.R.A. fishery finances

The prime direct source of fishery income is through fishing licence duties and, in some regions, through the levying of a fishery rate (whereby fishery owners or occupiers make a contribution to the N.R.A. based upon the value of their fisheries, a facility which has been strengthened under the Water Act 1989). In addition part of the general income of the N.R.A. and government finance is used for fishery and environmental purposes, the latter also indirectly benefiting fisheries.

1.6 Sea fisheries committees

Local S.F.C.s are established under the Sea Fisheries Regulation Act 1966 and draw their membership from local authority representatives and persons appointed by the Minister of Agriculture, Fisheries and Food. Their main source of income is a precept levied on the local authorities whose areas they are in. They are answerable in the final analysis to the Minister of Agriculture, Fisheries and Food who has the responsibility of approving any byelaw or order that they may wish to make to limit or control fishing in their areas.

Their powers extend out to the three mile limit and are concerned primarily with enforcing the size regulations for certain species of fish, shellfish and crustacea such as lobsters, crabs etc., and ensuring that any work proposed on the foreshore or in estuaries by outside bodies is not harmful to their interests.

As far as anglers are concerned they are only likely to come up against the S.F.C. representative if they foul hook fish, take undersized soft edible crabs for bait or retain sea fish which are below the minimum size limit.

The committees do not have bailiffs as such but may appoint fishery officers for the purpose of enforcing their byelaws – although the name is different the role is similar. Until the passing of the Salmon Act 1986 the fishery officers had no powers to act where salmon and migratory fish were involved, similarly bailiffs could not act where sea fish were involved. Now, however, both the N.R.A. and the S.F.C.s can make byelaws to control the use of instruments (which can and do prevent numbers of migratory fish ever reaching the river) in a sea fishery area provided the other body consents. This enables both bailiffs and sea fishery officers to enforce the relevant byelaws.

Chapter 2

FISHERY LAW IN ENGLAND AND WALES

2.1 The origins of fishery law

The fishery law of Great Britain - England, Wales and Scotland - probably originated in the pre-Norman era, when the country was split up into small kingdoms. Each king owned the land over which he ruled and laid claim to all game and fish found therein and in the waters adjoining. To protect these from poaching by serfs and varlets (and probably by his neighbours) he made laws to make certain things illegal and introduced penalties to help enforce them. These penalties were severe and included hanging.

When England at last, nominally, became united under one king the Royal Rights were challenged and, under Magna Carta, a public right of fishery in tidal waters was established. The need to keep rivers free from obstructions was recognised under later enactments. When England and Wales were eventually united under one monarch by the Act of Union of 1536 both countries enjoyed a common legal system including the public fishery rights established earlier.

Scotland in the meantime had continued to go its own way and existed as an independent feudal kingdom with its own laws and legal system that had evolved to meet the circumstances that existed there: these differed in many respects from those in England and Wales.

The Act of Union of 1707 joined Scotland to England and Wales to form the United Kingdom, but unlike the earlier Act of 1536 it allowed Scotland to retain much of its own law and legal system. Subsequent laws affecting the country, although made by a Parliament sitting in Westminster, were, for the most part, dependant upon the original Scottish legal system. Today many aspects of the common law, criminal law, civil law and the law of property apply only in Scotland and are unlike those found elsewhere in the United Kingdom. This difference is reflected in the law as it affects fisheries and fishing.

Under both the English and Scottish legal systems fishery laws evolved over many centuries and under changing regimes. In the process they safeguarded local interests, protected ancient rights and took steps to prevent fish stocks from being over exploited. Many of the earlier Acts related to specific rivers or areas giving rise to regional differences that extend into the present legislation and the common law.

Although the Scottish law has remained independent the problem of providing fisheries protection is basically the same as that south of the border. This is reflected in the provisions and powers under the various Acts now in operation. Although the intentions contained in the legislation under both systems are similar, wording, content and interpretation are often different and can be confusing to the angler.

Further confusion can arise over the law relating to fishery ownership in Scotland which differs considerably from that in England and Wales.

For these reasons Scottish law is dealt with separately in Part Two.

2.2 Divisions of the law

The law of England and Wales falls into two categories – common law and statute law.

Common law
This covers most of the law relating to fishery ownership and fishing rights. It has never been formally incorporated in any legislation, instead it has evolved over many centuries as a result of decisions arrived at by the courts. This is an on-going process whereby a present-day court decision can overturn previous rulings of an inferior court on a particular subject and that decision will hold good until such time that it in turn, is superseded or amended by a later decision of a superior court.

Statute law
Statute law is embodied in the Acts of Parliament and Statutory Orders which are made to serve a particular purpose – in the case of fisheries to protect fish, prevent over exploitation and to set up the organisation to ensure its implementation. As in the case of the common law, fishery statute law evolved through new and amending legislation to meet changing circumstances and attitudes (see Figure 2).

EVOLUTION OF FISHERY LAW

SALMON FISHERY ACT 1861
REPEALED 33 EARLIER
ACTS FROM THE TIME OF EDWARD I
TO QUEEN VICTORIA

SALMON AND FRESHWATER FISHERIES ACT 1923
TOTALLY REPEALED 18 ACTS FROM THE
SALMON FISHERY ACT 1861
TO THE
SALMON AND FRESHWATER FISHERIES ACT 1921

SALMON AND FRESHWATER FISHERIES ACT 1975
REPEALED:
THE WHOLE OF THE 1923, 1935, 1965 AND 1972 ACTS
AND
PARTS OF THE
WATER RESOURCES ACT 1963
COMPULSORY PURCHASE ACT 1965
WATER ACT 1973
CONTROL OF POLLUTION ACT 1974

SALMON ACT 1986
REPEALED PARTS OF THE 1975 ACT

WATER ACT 1989
REPEALED:
PARTS OF THE 1975 ACT

Figure 2

The 1975, 1981, 1986 and 1989 Acts are the latest in a long line of fishery legislation going back over many hundreds of years, the earliest of which was concerned with removing obstructions to fish and banning fishing at weekends. These two considerations have survived through the centuries and are still included in the current legislation, although the reason for banning weekend fishing has changed from what was originally probably a religious consideration to the present one of conservation.

In the intervening period many attempts have been made to update the law to take into account changes in needs and attitudes. All have met with varying degrees of success and all have revealed weaknesses – due largely to compromise, political expediency and bad drafting – that later legislation has attempted to rectify. The current Acts continue the process but, like their predecessors, they too have their faults and only time will tell if they achieve what they set out to do.

The Theft Act 1968 provides a link between the common and statute law in that it is, inter alia, concerned with the *protection* of the rights of fishery owners and occupiers.

Chapter 3

PUBLIC FISHERIES

3.1 Origin of public fisheries

Prior to Magna Carta all fishing rights both inland and around the coast, which included the foreshore (the coast between the high and low water marks of ordinary tides) and estuaries, were controlled by the king. In certain places the right to fish tidal waters was granted to a subject, usually for services rendered.

Magna Carta put a stop to this practice, took away the king's power and made fishing in tidal waters free for all, a situation that exists to this day. Therefore, as a generality a "public fishery" is one in which any member of the public has a right to fish and is synonymous with "tidal waters" which include sea, the foreshore and estuaries up to the tidal limit. But like most generalities there are exceptions. These are discussed below.

3.2 Private fisheries in tidal waters

Those tidal water fisheries granted to individuals by the king before Magna Carta were unaffected by it and remained the property of the grantees who in turn passed them onto their descendants.

With the passing of time these rights were disposed of and changed hands many times - often to persons who had no connection whatsoever with the original owners - but their status as private fisheries is as valid today as when the grants were originally made.

One private fishery exists in the tidal part of the River Usk in Gwent and others, which relate only to the use of instruments such as "putts and putchers", are found on both sides of the Severn Estuary.

All such fisheries, and others created later under statute (see below), now come under the heading of Private Fisheries (see page 17).

3.3 Creation of private fisheries in tidal waters

Although Magna Carta took away the right of the Crown to create private fisheries in tidal waters, such fisheries can still be created under certain Sea Fishery Acts and Regulations for the rearing and harvesting of different species of fish and such animals as oysters or mussels. Such a fishery belongs to the person to whom the fishery is granted under the appropriate Act.

3.4 Tidal and non-tidal boundaries

The boundary between tidal and non-tidal waters in a river, and therefore between public and private fisheries, is deemed to be the high tide limit of the ordinary tides. If a private fishery adjoins a public one this boundary will be shown on the deeds of the fishery.

As a rough guide, an angler fishing in a public fishery can find out where that fishery stops and a private one starts by reference to a $2\frac{1}{2}$ inch Ordnance Survey map where the tidal limit is marked.

3.5 Access to a public fishery

The right of the public to fish these waters usually includes the right to fish from the foreshore i.e. that part of the seashore which lies between the high and low water marks of ordinary tides – yet despite this, if the foreshore is only accessible by crossing private land above the high water mark, an angler may only be able do so – without meeting some form of constraint – from a boat. To cross this land without permission would be a trespass on the rights of the owner.

Local authorities who own and control the coast line, including piers and jetties, to which the general public are given a right of access, rarely impose any kind of restriction on where people can fish, but they would have the right to do so if they so wished. A beach, to which the public has free access, would not normally have any restrictions on its use by anglers.

3.6 Paying to fish in tidal waters

Under certain circumstances anglers may be asked to pay a fee to fish in tidal waters from properties which are owned by businesses or individuals. A case in point is where a charge is made for fishing off a pier. Similarly, in dockland areas a fee may be required from a person wishing to enter onto the property in order to fish.

The charge is not for the right to fish but for the right to use the property for that purpose and may be accompanied by a requirement that the angler observes any rules laid down as to method of fishing or conduct.

Usually there are no restrictions on angling from a boat for sea fish in a public fishery but the use of a rod and line or nets from a boat for salmon and sea trout fishing in such waters is strictly controlled by the N.R.A.

3.7 "Leasing" a fishery in tidal waters

Where a private fishery exists in tidal waters it may be possible to lease it, but such a possibility is rare and a club or individual who has managed to do so is indeed fortunate.

Some clubs claim to have the lease on a stretch of tidal water but it is more probable that what they have is a lease giving them the right of:-
(a) access to the water; and
(b) the use of the bank for fishing.

In such a case the club can prevent the use of the bank by an unauthorised angler, but this would not prevent anyone fishing from a boat or by wading upstream or downstream from part of the bank not controlled by the club.

3.8 Fishing from a public footpath

A public footpath only gives the public a right to pass to and fro along it, nothing else. This right does not imply ownership of the land by the public; in fact, most public footpaths cross private land and if any activity other than walking took place it could be a trespass against the landowner.

If the footpath runs along the edge of the bank of the tidal part of a river, where a public fishery exists, the public cannot, as a right, fish from it.

3.9 Setting nets in tidal waters

Although there is a public right of fishery in tidal waters this does not extend to the setting of nets on the foreshore which involves securing the net to the "soil". The foreshore belongs to someone and to use it to set a net without getting the owners consent would infringe his rights.

The setting of nets on the foreshore has led to a great deal of concern among anglers who turn up to fish only to find a net full of dead fish that have begun to rot or have been mutilated by birds.

S.F.C.s have the power to make byelaws to control the use of these nets and where byelaws have been made anyone contravening them would be liable to prosecution.

3.10 The control of fishing in tidal waters

While an angler has the right to fish in a public fishery this does not imply that he can fish in a way that contravenes any of the fishery legislation.

The enforcement of the legislation in tidal waters around the coast comes under three separate bodies:

(a) *Local sea-fisheries committees.*
The committees are responsible for enforcing the sea-fishery legislation out to a line three miles from the coast. The landward boundary is usually the high water line but it rarely extends into estuaries where, in the absence of an S.F.C., the N.R.A. can assume powers for regulating sea fishing.

Their control is minimal, but they do enforce minimum size limits in respect of certain species of fish. There are also byelaws in some areas to control abuses by anglers, in particular the foul-hooking of fish.

(b) *The N.R.A.*
The Authority is responsible for enforcing the provisions of the 1975, 1986 and 1989 Acts out to the six nautical mile fisheries' limit. It can also assume sea fishery powers in certain tidal waters not controlled by a S.F.C.

(c) *The Ministry of Agriculture, Fisheries and Food.*
This is responsible for enforcement between the six mile and twelve mile national limits.

The N.R.A. has power to make and enforce netting byelaws, and S.F.C.s. have similar powers in respect of nets and fixed engines, which relate to the taking, or obstructing the passage, of salmon and sea trout.

In addition to the above statutory bodies, local councils and possibly the Nature Conservancy Council may introduce byelaws affecting the foreshore which prohibit or regulate bait digging where it is deemed to be having a detrimental effect upon the natural fauna of the area.

3.11 Restrictions on fishing for sea fish

The legal restrictions on angling for sea fish from the shore are limited; however, minimum size limits, set by the Ministry, are enforced by the S.F.C.s.

Boat anglers may find more restrictions than the shore anglers. In recent years there has been a ban on the landing of such fish as cod taken from boats; this is part of the EEC quota scheme intended to prevent the overfishing of certain species considered to be threatened. Bass fishing from boats is now banned in certain areas. The areas affected vary from time to time and the unwary angler could be caught out if not careful.

3.12 Taking of salmon or sea trout at sea

It sometimes happens that an angler when fishing for sea-fish hooks and lands a salmon or sea trout – it is more likely to be the latter when he is spinning for bass or pollack near a river mouth.

If he holds the appropriate licence issued by the N.R.A., covering the area in which the fish was caught, and provided the fish was taken legally and in season, he would be entitled to keep it.

If none of the foregoing applied, and he kept the fish, he would risk prosecution if caught.

Chapter 4

PRIVATE FISHERIES

4.1 The origin of private fisheries

Originally all private fisheries on rivers lakes and ponds belonged to the king but were gradually disposed of to members of the nobility and persons whom the Crown wished to reward for their services. In turn, over the years, these were further disposed of, either in there entirety or as smaller and smaller fisheries, until today when the ownership in total is probably shared by tens of thousands of bodies or individuals.

Private fisheries are found in all non-tidal and inland waters. These include an estuary above the tidal limit, rivers, streams, canals, ponds, pools, ditches and reservoirs and, as stated earlier, in certain specific tidal waters. The rights associated with these fisheries can be owned by individuals, farmers, estates, angling clubs, syndicates, private companies, public corporations, local authorities, nationalised industries or the Crown who can exercise them in any way they choose.

All fisheries in non-tidal water belong to someone and although, in some cases, the rights associated with ownership may not have been exercised for many years the owner, once he has established his legal entitlement to do so, can utilise them in any way he wishes.

4.2 Presumptions as to ownership of a fishery

There are three presumptions in law relating to the ownership of a fishery to the adjoining land. These are:

(a) that the owner of the land adjoining a river owns the river bed up to the middle of the river;
(b) that the owner of the river bed owns the right to fish over it; and
(c) that the owner of the fishery owns the river bed below it.

These presumptions hold good except where it can be shown that at some time the right of fishery was separated from the land.

If a person buys the land which adjoins a river he is presumed to have become the owner of the fishery *unless the fishing rights are specifically excluded under the terms of the sale.* Likely causes for the fishery being excluded are that it is owned by someone else, or that the vendor wishes to retain the rights for himself.

4.3 The leasing or sale of a fishery

The property rights in land relate also to fisheries and as such they can be disposed of or used as the owner wishes. For example, if a person owns the fishing rights attached to his land he can lease or sell them, while still retaining the ownership of the land. What he disposes of is the "right to fish" only without any land being involved. This "right to fish" can apply to all species or to one species only, which could lead to a situation where, on the same fishery, one person owned the salmon fishing rights and another the coarse fishing rights.

The terms of a lease or conveyance usually include provisions relating to the use of the river bed up to the middle line of the river, access along the bank and access to and from the river.

Actual ownership or control of the bed and adjoining bank can only be achieved if the land is purchased or leased with the fishery. This would give the purchaser or lessee the right to prohibit or limit other activities associated with the use of the river which might otherwise interfere with his fishing.

4.4 Safeguards when leasing a fishery

It is a fact of life that if someone is offered something on the cheap he will jump at the chance if he wants it. This extends to acquiring fishing rights by individuals or clubs where the asking of a low rental is often linked to an informal agreement with an owner. Although this can be seen as an advantage under certain circumstances it does have considerable disadvantages compared with a tenancy based upon a formal lease drawn up by a professional person.

A formal lease safeguards the interests of both tenant and owner and guarantees occupancy of the fishery for a given time, which the informal agreement does not. The safeguards will depend upon what can be negotiated between the parties and will probably include provisions relating to some or all of the following, which the occupier would need:

(a) the right to fish,
(b) access along the banks,
(c) access to and from the water by agreed routes,
(d) work necessary to maintain the fishery,
(e) the removal of unwanted fish and to stock the water,
(f) numbers of anglers fishing at any one time, and
(g) the erection of a fishing hut or shelter.

This list can be added to or amended to suit individual requirements depending upon the circumstances and what the owner agrees to – he will also want certain safeguards which the tenant must agree to. An example of a fishery lease is given in Appendix B.

4.5 Fishery boundaries

When a fishery is bought or leased the deeds associated with the transaction should have a plan attached to them on which both the upstream and downstream limits of the fishery, the river boundary and the land over which access is permitted, will be shown. The three presumptions in law referred to on page 17 will apply unless anything to the contrary is included.

If the fishery is on both banks of a river the rights will extend over the whole width of the river. Where the fishery is confined to one bank only the boundary between it and that opposite will be the middle line of the river. In this case the boundary remains the middle line even if the river over the years gradually changes its course. This is why the boundary shown on an old deed will not necessarily be the same as it is at the present.

However, the boundary between two fisheries does not remain the middle line if there is a *sudden* change in the course of the river, as may occur after a very heavy flood or as the result of land drainage or river engineering works: under these conditions the boundary stays where it is and a person, who had rights on one bank only, may find that now he has them on both, while his neighbour opposite loses his rights in part or in total.

Fishing rights associated with one bank can extend across the whole width of the river, but not include the opposite bank. In this case the owner of the opposite bank will have no right to fish whereas the owner of the fishing rights can ignore the middle line presumption and wade over the whole width of the river in order to exercise them provided he does not use the opposite bank. Arrangements of this kind, when land or a fishery changes hands, can lead to misunderstanding between the parties on each bank and, to resolve it, the deeds relating to the fishery have to be consulted and each party made aware of the others rights.

4.6 The middle line of a river

Anglers are sometimes confused as to their rights when the fishery is confined to one bank only.

Strictly according to the law as the right of fishery ends at the middle line fishing is confined to that half of the river only but, despite some opinions to the contrary, most anglers are reasonable men and enter into a mutually acceptable agreement with the owner or tenant of the opposite fishery whereby both can fish over the whole width of the river provided that they do so from their own half. This commonsensical approach has been recognised in a recent Scottish court which decided that it should apply generally in Scotland but its validity in England and Wales has yet to be established.

When wading an angler has to be careful not to cross the middle line even if it is to fish his own half of the river. If he did so, either deliberately or by accident, he would be committing a trespass.

4.7 Defining banks

Some old deeds describe fisheries as being on "the north bank" or "south bank" of a river which is unsatisfactory if the river turns through 180° as the north bank then becomes the south and vice versa.

The current practice is to use the terms "left" or "right" bank determined when facing downstream. This enables the bank of a fishery to be identified irrespective of the direction in which the river is flowing.

4.8 Prescriptive rights

The right of an individual to fish on a particular piece of water or at a specific location can be acquired and established through longstanding usage as a "prescriptive" right. Such a right cannot be shared, passed on to a successor or be acquired by the public at large. It ceases on the death of the holder.

What constitutes "longstanding usage" and the establishment of a prescriptive right is usually a matter for the courts to decide.

4.9 "Bankers rights"

There is a belief in some places, based upon folk-lore rather than real law, that where a person lives on the bank of a river he can fish the water adjoining his property.

This belief is only supported when:

(a) the fishery owner exercises no control over his rights, or
(b) the fishery owner allows the property owner to fish, or
(c) the fishing rights form part of the property, or
(d) the property owner leases the fishing rights, or
(e) the property owner has a prescriptive right to fish, or
(f) the property adjoins tidal waters in which there is a public right of fishery.

If none of these conditions apply there is no right of fishery for anyone, whether he lives on the bank or not. The same conditions would apply to a lake, pond, reservoir or canal.

Conversely, the fishery owner may have a legal right to fish from the property of a person living on the bank of a fishery. It would depend upon the deeds relating to both the fishery and the property.

The above situation illustrates the need for ensuring that in any deed relating to property which has an adjoining fishery the situation and circumstances relating to both are clearly set out and understood. Occasionally, through an oversight, this is not done and the owner finds that he is denied a right of entry across or onto land adjoining part of the fishery. Consequently, the owner of this land may consider that he has "banker's rights" but he would be mistaken if none of the above conditions applied.

4.10 "Public" fisheries in non-tidal waters

The so-called "public" fisheries found on rivers, ponds, canals, etc. in various parts of the country are, in fact, not public at all but private fisheries. Because no one exercises any control over these waters or makes any charge for fishing them the public has assumed that the fishing is "public".

One likely reason for the lack of control of a fishery is that there is doubt as to who actually owns it; but the fact that no one exercises control does not extinguish the owner's right, once his title to the fishery is established, to manage or dispose of it in any way he or she wishes.

Pond fisheries found on common land are not open to the public at large but belong to the commoners – the local community with ancient rights to do such things as fish, graze sheep or cattle, cut peat, etc. – however, in many cases no control is exercised over these.

4.11 Fishing from a tow-path

A tow-path along a river bank is an indication that a right of navigation exists, which may be public or private, and that users of the navigation have a right to avail themselves of it for that purpose. The tow path does not indicate a public right of fishery and even if the water is tidal there is no automatic right for the public to use it for fishing from even though the fishery itself is public. Compare this to a footpath in tidal waters (See 3.8).

On the lower stretch of the river Thames, above the tidal limit, the public have been able to fish for many years from the tow-path without being required to have a permit, but in law they have no right to do so. The fact that they can is:

"by the indulgence or owing to the carelessness or good-nature of the person who is entitled to the soil, but right to fish themselves as the public they have none."

(This was the ruling in the case of *Blount* v *Lanyard* (1891)).

If the owners of the fisheries can establish their rights, which many may find difficult, there is nothing to prevent them from making a charge for fishing or exercising control in any way they wish.

Fishing from a tow-path without restraint may not extend to fishing in locks or from weirs associated with the navigation of a river. A permit is often needed for which a fee is payable.

Where a tow-path runs along the bank of a canal, although the navigation may be controlled by the British Waterways Board, or some other body, it does not necessarily control the fishery. In many places when the canals were being built the fishing rights were retained by the land owner and this still stands. The B.W.B. publishes a guide showing the waters it controls, issues permits and leases stretches of water, but generally restricts fishing to the tow-path only.

Where the fishing rights on a river or canal, with a tow-path along the bank, have been leased or sold, only the owner of those rights can fish – other legitimate users of the tow-path cannot do so; these remain the exclusive right of the fishery owner or tenant.

4.12 Fishing off bridges

A bridge carrying a road or railway which crosses a canal or river also crosses the fishing rights at that point; therefore, to fish from the bridge without permission is the same as fishing from the bank of the fishery and is illegal if one does not have permission from the owner or tenant of the fishery. In some cases the rights below a bridge belong to a highway authority but to fish legally permission is still needed.

Fishing from a road bridge could be an obstruction of the highway.

Where a bridge crosses the tidal part of a river it would not be an offence as the fishery would be public; however, there could be an infringement of the navigation byelaws or local authority byelaws.

Fishing from a railway bridge, either in a public or private fishery, can be an offence under the Railways Acts.

4.13 Fishing from a boat

When fishing from a boat an angler has precisely the same responsibilities, in the context of obtaining permission, as he would if fishing from the bank – this is often overlooked by anglers taking a boating holiday. The fishing rights, except in tidal waters, belong to someone and to fish without first having obtained permission is illegal. This implies, correctly, that anyone who takes a fishing rod with him on an inland boating holiday will be put to considerable trouble, to keep within the law, in getting permission from each fishery owner every time he moors his boat and wants to "have a dabble"!

On many stretches of canal and navigable river owned by British Waterways, the fisheries are managed directly; details of these, including maps and permit charges, are contained in an excellent guide issued by the Board.

There are other stretches of canal and navigable river controlled by clubs or individuals which display notices which inform the public that the fishing is private and it would be unwise to ignore them. Many clubs, however, are not only tolerant of, but also welcome boat anglers and provide for permits to be purchased on the waterside from their keepers.

4.14 Finding the ownership of private fisheries

Although all fisheries in non-tidal waters are private it is often difficult for a stranger to an area to find out who owns a particular stretch of water or where fishing is available to the casual angler. The best way, undoubtedly, is to ask someone in the locality who has obvious fishery connections such as a tackle shop or hotel proprietor. Other likely sources include the local angling community, estate agents, farmers and, in the case of canals, the British Waterways Board.

If intending to visit an area prior enquiries can be made through the local N.R.A. office, most of whom have Angling Guides for their areas, or by answering advertisements in the Angling Press. The Angling Guides not only give details of available fishing but also the addresses from which permits can be obtained.

If the owner of a fishery cannot be found or there is no indication that a fishery is private this does not imply that anyone can fish it without permission.

(See also Chapter 8 dealing with Fishing Permission.)

Chapter 5

FISHERY INTERFERENCE

5.1 Trespass

Trespass is by far the commonest form of interference to which a fishery can be subjected.

Trespass is a civil offence and is dealt with under the civil law where it is defined as:

"an unauthorised entry onto the land or property of others."

5.2 Dealing with trespassers

A person who is trespassing can be asked to leave a property and if he refuses the owner or tenant, or an agent of either, can use *reasonable* force to eject him. If the trespasser is fishing there are further powers which can be used; these are dealt with under "Fishing Permission" (See Chapter 8).

Trespass need not involve damage to property but if it does, redress can be sought through a civil court which has the power to make a defendant pay for any damage caused and, in the case of more persistent trespass, can grant an injunction which prevents him from continuing or repeating his actions.

5.3 Canoeing

Where a right of navigation exists canoeists and their crafts are entitled to use the water and there is little one can do to control their activities, if they interfere with the fishing rights, other than to appeal to their better nature. Navigation rights exist in tidal waters on certain rivers like the Severn, Thames, Trent etc. and on canals. On some other rivers navigation rights are in dispute and this often leads to conflict between anglers and canoeists.

Where there is no navigation right and where the canoeists have not received prior permission to use the water then it appears that they are trespassers and can be asked to leave. In many areas a good working relationship exists between the responsible canoe bodies, such as the British Canoe Union, and local angling interests. A major cause for concern in recent years has been the splinter groups of activists, and unattached canoeists who, in order to try and establish their rights, have antagonised the anglers by using the water without so much as "by your leave".

Difficulties can also arise when, for example, a farmer who owns the land gives permission for canoeing to take place without reference to the angling interests. This can be obviated at the time the lease or conveyance of the fishery is being discussed when a procedure to prevent such an eventuality can be formalised and included in the deed.

If the activities of canoeists on a non-navigable river cannot be dealt with by other means an injunction could be sought through the civil courts.

5.4 Bathing

The problems associated with bathers is similar to that caused by canoeing. Again the value of a good lease or conveyance is stressed.

5.5 Co-occupancy activities

The ownership or leasing of fishing rights does not preclude the use of the water for legitimate purposes by other persons who occupy the land adjoining the fishery even if these uses interfere with the fishing. The person from whom the fishery is purchased or leased will have rights which, if he is a farmer, will almost certainly include the watering of cattle in the river and possibly the removal of gravel.

Conversely, it should not be forgotten that the activities of anglers, if not properly controlled, can interfere with those of other legitimate water users.

In these circumstances there is little one can do to alleviate the situation other than to come to some mutual arrangement whereby both parties agree to limit their activities to times when the least interference will occur.

This again emphasises the need, when purchasing or leasing a fishery, for the appropriate safeguards to be incorporated in a properly drawn up agreement.

If in any doubt about the interpretation or implementation of the terms in such an agreement one should observe the golden rule – "seek professional advice".

5.6 Disturbance from river works

Under normal conditions any work carried out to the bed or banks of a river is liable to cause discoloration of the water for some distance downstream which can interfere with the pleasure of anglers.

If the work is of a major nature involving the use of heavy machinery and the removal of large quantities of material the disturbance could cause significant instability of the river channel. This in turn could lead to the transportation of bed material in times of flood into downstream fisheries, where holding pools could be silted up and good fishery habitat destroyed resulting in a loss of capital value of the affected fisheries.

It could be illegal under the Control of Pollution Act 1974 to start work of this kind without ascertaining the effect it would have both in physical and legal terms, and linked with this must be a process of consultation with all parties likely to be affected that should include:

(a) the N.R.A.;
(b) the local authority;
(c) the owner or tenants of the land on which the work is to be carried out;
(d) the owners or tenants of the downstream fisheries; and
(e) the downstream riparian owners;

Where possible any work should include provisions to minimise or compensate for any likely damage to the fishery and failure to reach prior agreement on this with those persons likely to be affected, before the work starts, could lead to later claims for compensation for damage to the fisheries.

Except in an emergency the N.R.A. is unlikely to do any work in a river without first carrying out the consultation process.

If the work is to be carried out by anyone other than the N.R.A. he will, at the outset, be required to consult with that body, as well as with the other interested parties if he wishes to avoid opposition. The river could be what is termed "main river" and any work in it will be subject to the approval of the Authority. If the river falls outside the definition of "main river", the

Authority may still wish to comment on the proposals, particularly if the location is used by salmon or trout for spawning purposes.

Any work carried out on any river, canal, watercourse pond or lake without N.R.A. consent which causes pollution could be a criminal offence under the Control of Pollution Act 1974.

5.7 Claims for damages arising from river work

Irrespective of whether any proposed river work is to be carried out by the N.R.A. or someone else, it is during the period of prior consultation that fishery owners or tenants must safeguard their interests by reaching an agreement with the body or person responsible for doing the work whereby it makes good or compensates for any subsequent deterioration or damage to the fishery. Any agreement should always be in writing.

A joint inspection of the fishery by all parties before the work starts, a comprehensive photographic record of the river and its banks, records of water depth taken at places most likely to be affected and an agreed statement of conditions that then exist, will establish the baselines for any future claims. Catch records for the fishery in the recent past can be used for the same purpose.

Claims for damages can be based upon loss of capital value and disturbance of the fishery. If a claim is contemplated the owner or tenant should be able to show that the income, e.g. from the sale of tickets, suffered because people were unwilling to fish in the conditions which existed during the time when the work was being carried out. A claim for loss of capital value should show that the fishery had suffered as a result of the work and that such things as holding pools, streams and lies which were essential for the maintenance of a good head of fish no longer existed.

5.8 Fishery "log-books"

The need to make a special effort to record the conditions of a fishery in order to claim for damages can be averted if the owner or tenant (especially one with a long lease) keeps a fishery log-book. This is used to record details of all catches, changes of flow and water depth, bank erosion, outside disturbance etc. – in fact anything which is relevant to the fishery.

An essential element is an accurate photographic record of the water when it is first taken over and further photographs to illustrate all changes.

One person is usually given the task of maintaining the record but all the fishery users are required to draw his attention to changes as they occur.

5.9 Dumping of tree branches into a water course

Rubbish and branches of trees deposited in a river can alter its regime and cause gravel to build up and flow patterns to change. This has an ongoing effect and can lead to the movement or disappearance of holding pools, cause flooding, create underwater hazards and encourage bank erosion, any of which will put an owner or tenant to some expense in order to rectify it.

If anyone throws any vegetation, such as tree branches, into a water course he could be guilty of an offence under section 49 of the 1974 Act. This states that:-

> "if without the consent of a water authority (N.R.A.), a person who cuts or uproots any substantial amount of vegetation in a stream, or so near it that it falls into it, leaves it to remain in the stream by wilful default he would be guilty of an offence."

and liable to a fine not exceeding £1000.

An examination of the upstream fisheries for signs of bank trimming will usually solve the question of where any material came from.

If the person responsible is known a "quiet word in his ear" might resolve the matter and lead to him removing the material. If this fails it should be reported to the N.R.A. who is responsible for enforcing this provision of the Act.

If the fishery suffered damage as a result of the rubbish the owner or tenant could make a claim against the offender which, as a last resort, could be pursued through the courts.

5.10 Bank erosion

Bank erosion is a condition which most fisheries experience to some degree at some time or another: under normal circumstances it is the responsibility of the owner or tenant to take whatever steps are necessary to rectify any damage and protect his property.

The N.R.A. will usually only deal with bank erosion as part of its responsibilities where it has a direct effect upon its functions.

If none are involved any erosion problem it agrees to deal with will probably be on a rechargeable basis.

5.11 Trees in a river

If a tree is washed down river and becomes lodged, causing an obstruction, the Authority would probably move this if it was interfering with the flow of the river or interfered in any way with its statutory functions.

5.12 Weirs and barriers

Any new weir or barrier in a river is subject to approval by the N.R.A. which would be unlikely to allow it to be built without insisting upon certain safeguards to allow fish to pass upstream. On migratory fish rivers any weir or other obstruction must have, under section 9 of the 1975 Act, an approved fish pass built into it.

Gauging weirs built by the Authority to monitor river flows are so designed that fish can swim over them.

Recently there have been a number of proposals put forward for the creation of water recreation areas, by impounding the water in river estuaries to form lakes, which has caused consternation in angling circles. These proposals are subject to scrutiny by and the approval of the N.R.A. and it is unlikely that they would be allowed to go ahead without all the implications, including those relating to fisheries, environment, flooding and pollution, being considered and possible dangers being obviated.

A barrier need not be physical – it can take the form of pollution. In the past, at the mouth of many rivers passing through heavily industrial areas pollution formed an impenetrable barrier to both the seaward and river migration of fish, but due to the various pollution prevention Acts and to the work of the N.R.A. and its predecessors, the water and river authorities, the problem has been greatly reduced.

Once a barrage has been built, and any detrimental effect it has can be proved by the upstream fishery owners, e.g. by salmon and seatrout being prevented from moving up river, they could have a claim against the person or body responsible.

Anything which interferes with the movement of fish can be considered to be a barrier. In one case a power station built on the estuary of a river killed many thousands of salmonid smolts by sucking them into the cooling water intake. Once this had been drawn to the attention of the electricity authority it compensated the fishery owners by building a hatchery to make up for the losses sustained and introduced an annual "smolt rescue" operation.

5.13 The introduction of alien species of fish

The appearance of an unwanted species of fish in an established fishery is worrying especially if it poses a danger to the indigenous species or threatens to change the nature of the fishery.

Strange species can appear in a water through natural processes such as the transfer of ova or fry in weed attached to the feet of birds but in most cases a more likely explanation is that someone has introduced them, and if this was done without the consent of the N.R.A. an offence would have been committed. Consent is unlikely to be given to the introduction of a species that would be detrimental to the present population or change the character of the fishery.

If a deliberate illegal stocking is suspected the Authority should be informed immediately and an investigation started by it to discover the person responsible. If such evidence is available then the culprit can be prosecuted in the courts and faces a maximum penalty, if found guilty, of £1000.

The Authority may be able to help remove the fish but the chances of completely removing them all are remote. However, if the remaining numbers are very small they may eventually die out due to competition from, or predation by, the native fish.

A fishery whose character is changed as the result of the appearance of an alien species can deter anglers who have fished there in the past from doing so in the future resulting in a financial loss. If this can be attributed to a particular person then the owner or tenant can make a claim against him under the civil law.

(See also Chapter 14 dealing with Stocking and Moving Fish).

Chapter 6

POLLUTION

6.1 Definition

Under the common law a riparian or fishery owner is entitled to receive river water in its natural state and is required to let that water flow in the same condition to his neighbours downstream.

Any thing added to the water to change its character or quality is a "pollution" and a riparian owner who experiences such a change due to the activity of another person upstream should be able to proceed against that person under the common law.

Also, under the various pollution prevention Acts a pollution can be any discharge, the quality of which fails to comply with the conditions contained in a consent issued by the N.R.A., that enters a water course. This would be a statutory criminal offence.

Section 4 of the 1975 Act makes it an offence for:

"any person to cause or knowingly permit to flow, or put or knowingly permit to be put, into any waters containing fish or into any tributaries of water containing fish, any liquid or solid matter to such an extent as to cause the waters to be poisonous or injurious to fish or the spawning grounds, spawn or food of fish."

It is the duty of the N.R.A. to enforce this section and to proceed against offenders, but the section goes on to say that;

"any person who has first obtained a certificate from the Minister that he has a material interest in the waters alleged to be affected"

can also take proceedings against a polluter.

6.2 Kinds of pollution

Of all the forms of interference that a fishery can experience pollution is probably the most emotive and potentially disastrous. Not only are fish killed but in many cases the fishery is rendered sterile or un-fishable for a considerable time.

Pollution can take many forms including:-

(a) toxic matter which acts upon the organs of the fish and kills them e.g. cyanide;

(b) de-oxygenating matter which kills fish by removing the oxygen from the water e.g. silage liquor;

(c) suspended matter which can choke the gills of fish and cut off sunlight thereby interfering with the food chain e.g. sand or coal washery effluents; and

(d) radio activity which can interfere with the genetic make up of the fish.

Even when the cause of the pollution stops it may take many months for the river to cleanse itself and even longer for the fish and their food organisms to re-establish themselves.

6.3 Evidence of pollution

Proving that a pollution has occurred, and who has caused it, necessitates the gathering of evidence.

Probably the first sign of a pollution noticed by an angler is the discoloration of the river or pond and/or the appearance of dead or dying fish. It is at this time, when the likely cause of the pollution is obvious, that the best evidence can be collected.

Although the N.R.A. is responsible for investigating pollutions, by the time it has been notified and arranged for an officer to visit the site vital time will have passed and the evidence much more difficult to collect.

This is where the angler who spots the pollution can help. If possible he should take samples of any discharge suspected of causing the pollution and of the river above and below the discharge point. He should also collect samples of as many fish as possible and take a further sample of the water from the area where the fish were found.

If the source of the pollution is not obvious only the latter samples need be taken.

Water samples should be taken in clean bottles which presupposes that the angler will have such bottles with him! In most cases he will not but it is surprising what can be pressed into service to collect samples when the need arises – the main consideration is that they be clean.

Once samples have been taken, contact the local office of the N.R.A. giving your name and address, details of the location and arrange to meet an officer at a specific place (in most regions there is an emergency number given in telephone directories under "Water").

When the officer arrives hand him the samples of fish and water and tell him what you saw. He will probably require you to make a written statement.

6.4 The incident report

In addition to any action which the N.R.A. might take against the polluter the owner or tenant of the fishery will probably wish to claim against him for damages. If the case has to be decided by a court the proceedings may not be heard until many months after the incident – and during this time the memory of the person discovering it and taking samples can become blurred which does not help if that person is called to give evidence. To avoid this embarrassment it is always advisable, in these circumstances, for the person concerned to make a written report as soon as possible of what he actually saw and did. This can be used later to refresh his memory.

6.5 Claiming for pollution damage

Depending upon the strength of the evidence and other factors the Authority may decide to prosecute the polluter and, if found guilty, he faces a heavy fine in a criminal court. Sometimes the polluter offers to re-stock the affected fishery or fisheries – but is not usually required to do so by the court who hears the case against him.

Any claim for damages must therefore be made against the polluter by the owners or tenants of the affected fisheries. The claim could be for a cash settlement or the re-stocking of the fishery. To substantiate a claim the value of loss sustained must be carefully assessed to include both the numbers and monetary value of adult fish, immature fish and fry. Also consideration must be given to the loss of natural fish food and spawning potential.

In addition, if the pollution causes a loss of income because there are no fish for anglers to catch a figure to cover this must be included in the claim. One way of calculating this is by comparing the income during the season when the pollution occurred with that of the previous two seasons.

Most compensation claims are settled only after long negotiations but even then no agreement may be reached. The plaintiff, i.e. the fishery owner or tenant, is then faced, as a last resort, with asking the civil court to resolve the matter. This will require proving to the satisfaction of the court that the defendant had caused the pollution in the first place. This is often more difficult than at first appears but guidance and help can be provided by the Anglers' Cooperative Association, which operates nationally to protect the interests of fishery owners and occupiers against pollution and to support its members in claims for compensation.

Where a major pollution occurs affecting a number of fisheries any claim is best dealt with by all concerned acting in concert.

Chapter 7

PREDATION

7.1 Natural interference

Most of the interference with fisheries discussed so far has been man-made, but there are natural factors which are also alleged to affect fisheries adversely, one of the principal factors being predation by birds and animals.

This is a very emotive subject on some rivers and figures have been produced to suggest that large numbers of immature salmonids are taken each year by birds, such as cormorants and goosanders, leading to a decrease in fish stocks. It is not intended that the pros and cons of the arguments be discussed here, instead the legal position relating to all natural fish predators is examined.

7.2 Predation by birds

Cormorants, herons and various species of duck feed almost exclusively on fish, but do not confine their activities to natural wild fish. Rivers and lakes stocked artificially and fish-holding ponds provide the opportunity for easy meals, much to the consternation of those responsible for the fisheries, which in the past has led to the demise of many birds at the hands of a man with a gun.

In the past, under the Protection of Birds Act 1954 birds such as cormorants, feeding on fish in a river or lake, could be killed legally at any time by an "authorised person". In this context the authorised person would have been the owner or tenant of the fishery or any other person authorised by either. This has now changed.

Under the Wildlife and Countryside Act 1981 which superseded the 1954 Act, most predatory species of bird that feed on fish are given protection and it is an offence to kill them.

However there is a provision in the Act which allows the Minister of Agriculture (or the Secretary of State in the case of Wales) to issue a licence which will allow a person with a direct interest in a fishery to shoot cormorants, goosanders, great crested grebes, black headed gulls, common gulls, herons, mergansers, shags and common terns *if he can show that they are causing serious damage to the fish stocks.*

An application for a licence should be made in the first instance to the nearest divisional office of the Ministry of Agriculture, Fisheries and Food (as listed in the telephone directory) which can also give further guidance on the workings and interpretation of the Act.

The Minister or Secretary of State will not usually grant licences without reference to the Nature Conservancy Council which advises on their issue. The N.R.A. and any other body with an apparent interest may also be consulted, some may have adopted a policy to protect such birds and this could influence the Minister or Secretary of State on whether or not to issue a licence.

7.3 Degrees of protection

All those species named above are protected and a maximum fine of £400 can be imposed by a court for killing one illegally and intentionally.

Other species including all species of diver, kingfisher and osprey are specially protected and given absolute protection by the law. If one of these is killed the maximum penalty is £2000.

Some species of gull (black backed and herring) are not given any protection and may be killed by an authorised person which in the case of a fishery would be the owner or tenant.

The full details of all the species and the various degrees of protection they are given are contained in the Wildlife and Countryside Act 1981, copies of which can be obtained from H.M. Stationery Office. An excellent and very readable booklet "Predatory Birds of Game and Fish" published by the British Field Sports Society summarises parts of the Act and contains all the information that a fishery owner would require, including ways of preventing damage by bird predators.

7.4 Emergency action

If a cormorant gained access to a hatchery pond filled with thousands of small fish it would be impractical to wait for a licence to be issued before the matter could be dealt with – all the fish could have been eaten in the meantime. In this case, because of the special circumstances, the owner could take immediate action to kill the bird *but there must be sufficient evidence to show a court that the action was necessary to prevent serious damage.* It would be advisable to notify both the local office of the Ministry and the Nature Conservancy Council, as soon as possible, of the action taken as this may prevent the matter going any further.

7.5 Otters

The loss of a few trout – and probably a lot of eels – is a small price to pay for the presence of an otter on a fishery. An owner or tenant should consider himself very lucky to have the animal gracing his water, for the otter is extremely rare, its numbers having declined dramatically over much of Great Britain during the last few decades. At one time, in the not too distant past, the otter was hunted with hounds but this practice has now been banned by law. Many fishery owners, who once supported the hunt in the mistaken belief that by so doing they were protecting their fish stocks, are now actively concerned with protecting the otter and by cooperating in the creation of "otter havens" intended to encourage the re-establishment of the animal in areas it once frequented.

Under no circumstances should anything be done that would endanger the animal as it is now heavily protected by law and to kill or injure it carries a heavy penalty.

7.6 Mink

Mink became part of the fauna of this country some thirty years ago when a few escaped from farms where they were being reared for their skins. Since then they have increased greatly in numbers and spread to most parts of the country where, because they feed on fish, birds and small mammals, they are regarded as pests. Consequently they are not protected by the law and can be trapped or shot in an effort to keep them under control. Any trap used must be of an approved design – to use a trap such as a gin is illegal and carries a heavy penalty. The local pest control officer or the Ministry of Agriculture, Fisheries and Food can advise on the best method of trapping.

7.7 Predatory fish

The numbers of predatory fish such as pike, and sometimes perch and zander, can increase to such an extent that they threaten the other species found in a fishery – this is especially true in trout fisheries. When it can be shown that these conditions exist the removal of all or part of the predatory population may help towards restoring the fishery to its former condition, but to do so without first obtaining the approval of the N.R.A. could be illegal.

Under certain circumstances the Authority will permit the use of instruments or methods, which would otherwise be prohibited, to remove fish considered to be injurious to a fishery. These include the use of a snare, set-line, spear, gaff, stroke-haul, snatch and electro fishing equipment.

Application should be made in writing in which the applicant must specify the instrument or method that he wishes to use and the species of fish he wants to remove. He must also satisfy the Authority that its use is intended for the preservation or development of the fishery.

The instrument or method must not be used until permission in writing has been given, otherwise the person using it could face a maximum penalty of three months in prison, a fine of £2000 or both.

Chapter 8

FISHING PERMISSION

8.1 Legal requirement

The owner or tenant of a fishery can exercise his right to fish on that fishery at any time (subject to any legal requirements) and can allow anyone else to do so under any conditions he wishes to make, including the payment of a fee. These conditions can be of great importance as will be shown later.

Conversely, anyone wanting to fish that fishery must first seek and obtain the permission of the owner or tenant.

In addition, both the owner or tenant of the fishery and any person fishing it, or any other fishery, will need a valid N.R.A. licence, purchased before he starts to fish (see Chapter 10).

8.2 Angling clubs

Probably the easiest way to obtain permission to fish is by joining an angling club. Most cater for the anglers in the immediate vicinity and have at least one lake, pond or stretch of river within easy reach which their members can fish. Others own or control fisheries of widely varying quality and interest in many parts of the country which provide a diversity of sport at the minimum of cost, even to a casual angler.

By joining a club the member automatically has access to all waters unless the rules provide otherwise. The same facilities are usually offered to an angler who does not join the club but buys a permit to fish.

In many parts of the country anglers are well served by clubs, and may have a number to choose from, whereas elsewhere they are few and far between, especially on some of the better game fish rivers, where the majority of the fisheries are controlled by individuals or syndicates.

Some enterprising local authorities have developed or created fisheries for the benefit of all as part of their recreational commitment. These can either be fished free of charge or on payment of a small fee.

If not a club member or holder of a club permit an angler wishing to fish other waters will have to seek out the owner or tenant of the fishery he wants to fish and obtain permission.

8.3 Obtaining permits

Provided that a fishery is available to the public, permission to fish it can be obtained by the purchase of a fishing permit which can be obtained from the owner, occupier or an agent, including fishing tackle shops, post offices, etc.

Depending upon the type and quality of the fishery, permits for one day can cost anything from a few pence to several pounds.

The permit should be purchased before fishing starts and carried by the angler when fishing.

In some places a permit can be bought on the bank from a club official or keeper after the angler has started fishing, but this system has a weakness – an angler will not have the opportunity, (or perhaps not attempt) to buy a permit unless he is asked to do so by the permit seller. For this reason the practice is now less popular than it was.

A word of caution needs to be made here – if anyone comes up to an angler on the bank of a fishery and asks him for payment to fish the water always ask that person to provide proof of his identity and authority for seeking payment. If no proof is forthcoming do not hand over any money.

When purchasing the permit the angler should take the opportunity to ask for details about the fishery and, in particular, what rules apply. The permit is issued subject to the angler complying with the conditions laid down in the rules: these are either printed on the permit or issued separately – failure to observe them could have serious consequences (see page 50).

8.4 The permit

Permits, which give the holder the authority to fish, come in all shapes and sizes but all conform to a basic pattern. The following example is typical and contains most of the information one would expect to find on any permit.

THE COLLYWOBBLE CARP CLUB

PERMIT No. 1234

Mr...

Address..

....

is authorised to fish all waters owned by the club

for a period of .....day(s)

commencing on..................

and ending on..................

THIS PERMIT IS ISSUED SUBJECT
TO THE HOLDER COMPLYING WITH THE RULES OF THE CLUB
(See back of permit)

Fee paid £..........

Issued at.......a.m./p.m.

on the........day of.........19..

.... Issuing Agent

(The reference to the rules of the club implies that, if this had been a real permit, they would have been printed on the back).

8.5 The difference between a permit and a licence

Many people get confused between a permit and a licence and what each entitles them to do. The main characteristics of each are as follows:

(a) A fishing permit;
    (i) is granted by a fishery owner or occupier,
    (ii) entitles the holder to fish a specific fishery only,

(iii) usually allows the holder to fish for all species of fish,

(iv) is non-statutory but provides proof of entitlement to fish,

(v) must be produced on demand to the fishery owner, his agent or a constable, and

(vi) is *not* a substitute for a fishing licence.

(b) A fishing licence;

(i) is issued by the N.R.A.,

(ii) applies to rivers or areas shown on the licence,

(iii) is valid only for the species of fish specified,

(iv) is a statutory requirement,

(v) must be produced to a water bailiff, constable or other licence holder, and

(vi) can only be used where the holder has permission to fish.

8.6 Duration of permits

The period for which a permit can be issued will depend upon the policy adopted by the fishery.

Some clubs insist on anyone wishing to fish becoming a full member, in which case his right to fish will remain for as long as he remains a member.

Other fisheries will issue season or shorter period permits to anyone who applies. The shortest term is usually for one day but some high quality reservoir trout fisheries cater for half-day or evening fishing also.

The latest trend on some of the more heavily stocked trout fisheries is to issue a permit at a flat rate but to charge the angler on the weight of the fish he catches – for which there is usually a limit on the number. When this is reached the permit has to be renewed.

8.7 Transfer of permits

Most fisheries make it one of the conditions of the sale that permits issued are non-transferable, but there are exceptions. Some fisheries which are very popular with anglers have to ration day permits and to ensure they get one anglers will often book up in advance. When subsequent events prevent the angler using his permit a telephone call to the fishery will usually result in him being allowed to transfer the permit to a nominated person.

Season permit holders on other fisheries may be allowed to let guests use their permits on limited occasions, provided advance notice is given. Other fisheries allow season permit holders to invite a guest to fish on a limited number of occasions. Usually the guest must be accompanied by the permit holder or, if not, he must be in possession of a note from the permit holder to the effect that he is his guest.

8.8 Permit production

As a permit is the only proof that an angler has of his right to fish, it must be carried by him at all times when fishing on the water to which the permit applies. The angler can be asked to produce his permit by anyone with a legitimate interest in the fishery such as the owner or occupier, a keeper, or other angler holding a valid permit, who suspects that he is fishing without permission. A requirement that an angler produces his permit on request should be included in the rules of all fisheries. This will help overcome the resentment shown by some anglers when asked to do so.

As a matter of policy an angler should always check the credentials of anyone he does not know who purports to be acting on behalf of a fishery owner or tenant and should always ask for proof of identity when required to produce a permit or licence.

8.9 Powers of a keeper to inspect permits

One of the principle tasks of a fishery keeper is to ensure that no one fishes without permission and to this end he can require anyone who is fishing there to provide proof of his entitlement to do so and to produce a permit.

In this role he acts on behalf of the owner or occupier who should provide him with an identity document to provide proof of who he is and whom he represents. Ideally such a document should include a photograph of the holder.

If the keeper produces a valid *fishing licence* he can demand to see the *licence* of an angler who does not have a permit, or ask for his name and address, under section 35 of the 1975 Act. Provided the angler has a licence and produces it, and should the need arise, his name and address can be obtained from it. If he refuses to comply with the request the matter should be reported to the N.R.A.

If the angler does not have a valid permit he is a trespasser and the keeper has the power to require him to leave the fishery and if the angler refuses to go the keeper can use reasonable force to eject him. This power is reinforced under the Theft Act 1968 which gives any member of the public the right to seize a rod or tackle being used by someone fishing without permission on a private fishery.

Under certain circumstances the Theft Act allows the arrest of a person. However, an arrest should not be made unless one knows how to set about it, and then only as a last resort. Misuse of the power could result in a charge of assault or unlawful arrest being laid against the person making the arrest.

Powers under the Theft Act are dealt with in more detail later.

The N.R.A. can also appoint keepers, and others, as honorary water bailiffs. They have the same powers as full-time water bailiffs but, in that capacity, only in relation to offences committed under the 1975 Act, *not* the Theft Act.

8.10 Powers of anglers to inspect permits

An angler with a legitimate right to be fishing a water has the same powers, in relation to anyone fishing without permission, as those of the keeper discussed above, but he may find difficulty in enforcing them if he has no documentary proof of his rights to do so. Some angling clubs overcome this by printing on the permit that the holder has the right to inspect the permit of anyone else seen fishing. If a person suspected of fishing without permission refuses to produce a permit the angler should make a note of his appearance and description and pass the information to the fishery owner, occupier or Club officials for any action they may wish to take.

8.11 Permit inspection by a constable

Fishing without a permit is an offence under the Theft Act (See Chapter 9) and as such a constable who suspects an angler of committing an offence by fishing without permission can have his suspicions allayed by the production of a valid permit.

8.12 Permit inspection by a water bailiff

Although the powers of water bailiffs do not include the right to inspect permits, they have a right to do so when a permit also covers a licence fee.

Where a fishery operates under a "General Licence" (i.e. a licence issued by the N.R.A. to the owner of the fishery, which covers all persons fishing on it), an angler need not have an individual fishing licence. His entitlement to be on the water is his permit which is also proof that he is covered by the general licence and therefore licensed to fish by the N.R.A. Under these circumstances the permit can be demanded for inspection by a water bailiff.

On some fisheries, if an angler is unable to produce a valid licence when he buys his permit, he can buy a day licence but instead of having a separate document issued he will have his permit endorsed to the effect that he has purchased a licence. The permit is then proof that he is licensed and, therefore, is subject to inspection by a water bailiff.

On reservoirs and other fisheries retained in the ownership of the N.R.A. after the privatisation of the water industry under the 1989 Water Act, where permits to fish are issued, water bailiffs can ask to inspect the permits. They do so not by virtue of any of their powers but as employees of the N.R.A.

Chapter 9

FISHING AND THE THEFT ACT

9.1 The ownership of fish

Whether or not fish in a river or pond are the property of any person depends upon where they are found – in most cases it will be seen that they belong to no one!

As a general rule the position can be set out as follows:-

(a) Where a pond or any enclosed water, *unconnected to any water course*, is surrounded by land, the land under the pond, the water and any fish it contains belong to the owner of the land. This can be extended to fish farm ponds and garden pools where the fish are physically and artificially contained within a body of water. If the property is sold ownership of the fish passes to the purchaser unless there is anything to exclude them from the terms of the sale.

Fish meeting the above condition belong to someone and are therefore capable of being stolen.

(b) In running waters which form part of or are connected to a river system (e.g. rivers, canals, ditches and lakes with water running through them), where fish can move freely from one fishery to another, *the fish are deemed to be wild creatures and as such to belong to nobody*. If a person introduces fish into these waters by way of stocking, his ownership of the fish is forfeited once they have been placed in the water as they are then considered to have been released into the wild and to have become wild creatures – as such they belong to nobody!

9.2 The theft of fish

If the ownership of the fish can be established e.g. by the owner of a fish farm, then any person who takes them without permission will have committed theft, defined under section 1 of the Theft Act 1968 as:

"the dishonest appropriation of property belonging to another with the intention of permanently depriving the other of it"

On conviction on indictment (in the Crown Court) for an offence under this section a person would be liable to a term of imprisonment not exceeding 10 years.

The offence could also be heard by a magistrates' court. Here the maximum sentence which might be imposed is not as severe as that of the higher court but if the offender was found guilty of the offence he could be sent to the Crown Court for sentence if the magistrates were of the opinion that the nature or magnitude of the offence merited a heavier penalty than they were able to award.

In most cases involving the theft of fish the matter is referred to the police who investigate the offence and prosecute the offender.

9.3 Schedule 1(2) of the Theft Act 1968

As has been shown, fish that are wild creatures cannot be stolen, but nevertheless the law makes provision to prevent them being taken illegally from private fisheries.

Because wild fish belong to nobody they cannot be stolen, but if one is caught it becomes the property of the captor and even if the person catching the fish has no right to be fishing the water, he cannot be accused of the theft of the fish because it belonged to no one and, as a general rule, one cannot steal anything which has no owner!

To close this loop-hole schedule 1(2) of the 1968 Act creates the offence of taking fish illegally in private waters. This states that:-

"Any person who unlawfully takes or destroys or attempts to take or destroy any fish in water which is private property or in which there is a private right of fishery shall on summary conviction be liable to imprisonment for a term not exceeding three months or a fine not exceeding £400 or both."

The term "unlawfully" in this context is taken to mean without lawful authority i.e. without permission.

It should be noted that this schedule refers to "fish". The significance of this is that it applies to any species, including seafish, some species of which can, and do, enter rivers (e.g. flounders, shad, mullet) and anyone unlawfully taking such fish in a private fishery would be caught by the Act.

The other important feature is that the offence can only be committed "*in water which is private property or in which there is a private right of fishery"* – in other words there can be no offence in a public fishery. As a general rule there are no private fisheries in tidal waters and therefore the Act cannot apply. However, in those exceptional places where a private fishery can be shown to exist the provisions of the Act do apply; thus anyone stealing oysters from a private fishery in tidal waters would be caught by the Act.

The schedule goes on to state that:

"The above shall not apply to taking or destroying fish by angling in the day-time but a person who by angling in the day-time (that is in the period beginning one hour before sunrise and ending one hour after sunset) takes or destroys or attempts to take or destroy any fish in water which is private property or in which there is a private right of fishery shall on summary conviction be liable to a fine not exceeding £50."

This, in effect, creates a separate offence of angling in the day-time and carries with it a lesser penalty than that which could be imposed for angling at night or using other methods of fishing at any time.

It should be noted that an angler fishing at night on a private fishery without permission places him in the position of being treated exactly the same as any other poacher (see below).

In the above, the offences are set out and in order to give effect to the enforcement of most of its provisions of the Act, the schedule goes on to provide the means whereby offenders can be apprehended and makes provision for the forfeiture of any instrument or fish. It states:-

"The court by which a person is convicted of an offence may order the forfeiture of anything which at the time of the offence he had with him for taking or destroying fish and that any person may arrest without warrant anyone who is or whom he has reasonable cause to suspect of committing an offence (other than angling during daylight) under this schedule, and any person may seize from any person who is or whom he has reasonable cause to suspect of committing any offence under this schedule anything which on that person's conviction would be liable to be forfeited by a court."

The power of arrest (but not for angling in the day-time) is given as is the power to seize tackle and fish but note that it is only the court that can make an order forfeiting anything seized.

*Under this schedule it is not necessary for an angler to have caught
a fish to be guilty of an offence; his mere presence on the water
attempting to take fish is itself an offence.*

9.4 Seizure of tackle under the Theft Act

Unless a person purporting to exercise his powers under this
Act can provide evidence of his identity and status, in the form
of a warrant or authority from an employer, an angler should
never hand over to him any tackle, fish or other item. However,
any member of the public can seize tackle used unlawfully under
the Theft Act and such a person may well have no written
authority.

*If the person intending to seize the tackle cannot substantiate his
right to do so the angler would be advised not to hand it over immediately
but to accompany his accuser to a police station and hand it over there
in exchange for a receipt, in the presence of a police officer.*

9.5 Fishery rules and the Theft Act

The terms of a permit are paramount and in being granted permission to fish, either verbally or by the purchase of a permit,
the angler enters into a contract with the owner or occupier
whereby he agrees to observe the rules of the fishery in exchange
for the right to fish. If the angler breaks any of the rules, e.g.
by using a prohibited bait or method, he is in breach of his contract,
his permit is invalidated and he becomes a trespasser (which is
a "civil" not a "criminal" offence). However, as a trespasser he
would be fishing unlawfully when the provisions of the Theft
Act would apply. Thus the use of part of criminal law can be
used to enforce the rules of a fishery – this usually has a far
more salutary effect upon an offender than his being banned
from the fishery.

9.6 Fish caught contrary to the rules

If the rules of the fishery permit it, any fish caught can be kept
by the angler. Some fisheries lay down a "bag limit" – if this is
exceeded the angler would have broken the terms of his permit
and committed an offence under the provisions of the Theft Act.
    The removal or killing of any fish by anglers is sometimes
prohibited on coarse fisheries, instead, anglers are required to

return to the water immediately any fish caught, or if a keep net is used, at the end of the day. Again, failure to observe this could be an offence.

Similarly if the rules lay down a minimum size limit and fish less than this are taken and killed, or baits methods of fishing which are prohibited are used, the angler lays himself open to a Theft Act offence.

9.7 The validity of warning notices

Notices erected on fisheries drawing the attention of the public to the fact that a fishery is private using the words "TRESPASSERS WILL BE PROSECUTED" have little value in law. As explained earlier a trespass is a *civil* matter whereas the term "prosecution" relates to the *criminal law*. It is, therefore, not possible to "prosecute" a person for trespass.

A more desirable form of wording would read as follows:-

COLLYWOBBLE CARP CLUB

PRIVATE FISHING

Any person found fishing on these waters without the written permission of the above Club is liable to prosecution under Schedule 1 (2) of the Theft Act 1968.

Signed:-Joe Bloggs

Club Secretary

This makes it clear that any offence will be dealt with under criminal law, it also makes it much easier to deal with in the context of any legal proceedings.

Notices should be placed at the upstream and downstream limits of a river fishery and elsewhere on any fishery where the public can gain easy access to the water.

In view of the possibility of vandalism any notice board should be made of metal or heavy plastic. Although expensive initially, strong material is more economical in the long run.

9.8 Dealing with "rule breakers"

When an allegation of a breach of the fishery rules is acted upon by the aggrieved party it can be argued that an unbiased decision as to the "punishment" of the offender may be difficult to arrive at. Consequently, a club or fishery owner who bans a person from fishing could be accused of defaming that person's character if it could be shown that the action taken was unwarranted, unfair or malicious and that his reputation suffered as a result. This situation cannot arise if the offender is prosecuted under the Theft Act as the rights and wrongs of the case will be decided by an independant arbitrator – the 'court.

The use of this Act by owners and tenants, especially angling clubs, to deal with unauthorised fishermen and rule breakers is often ignored as many people believe that the costs involved in taking the case to court outweigh any benefit that they might gain, but the court which finds an offender guilty can be asked to make an order for all or part of the prosecution costs to be met by the defendant. Incidentally, it is not always necessary to use the services of a lawyer to prosecute a poacher, the owner or occupier of the fishery can do it himself if he knows the procedure, but if in doubt always go to a solicitor.

It could be claimed by a person prosecuted under this Act that he committed the offence because he was unaware of the relevant rule and, although ignorance of the law is not a excuse, this might be accepted in terms of mitigation. To overcome this possibility fishery rules should be prominently displayed at the point where permits are sold or they should be printed and a copy given with every permit issued.

Chapter 10

LICENCES

10.1 The need for a rod licence

A rod licence is a legal requirement. Under section 25 of the 1975 Act the N.R.A. is obliged to issue licences for fishing for salmon and trout. It must also issue licences for fishing for freshwater fish *unless excused by the Minister*.

Strictly, the term "rod licence" is a misnomer. If it was a "rod licence" in the true sense of the term it would imply that anyone could use a specific rod for which a licence was issued.

The licence issued to an angler licenses him, as an individual, to fish with (usually) *any* single rod and line – however, as the term "rod licence" is in general use it will be used henceforth.

In addition, a rod licence authorises the holder to use a gaff, tailer or landing net as an auxilliary to the use of any rod and line.

The prime reason for issuing licences is to raise revenue to enable the fisheries function of the Authority to be financed, but licences also serve other purposes e.g. to provide proof that an angler is licensed, to monitor the numbers of anglers, and help to prevent unrestricted exploitation of the fisheries.
The licence revenue helps to finance:-

(a) a water bailiffing force,
(b) the monitoring of fish stocks,
(c) the maintenance of fish rearing facilities,
(d) the reinstatement of neglected fisheries,
(e) the creation of new fisheries,
(f) the protection of angling interests against interference, and
(g) the general maintenance, improvement and development of the fisheries.

10.2 Eligibility to hold a rod licence

The N.R.A. is obliged to issue a rod licence to any person who applies for one provided that at the time of the application that person was not disqualified from holding one.

A person found guilty of an offence under the 1975 Act can have his current licence withdrawn by the court and be disqualified from holding a licence for up to five years. This could be in addition to any other penalty that the court may impose.

N.B. It is *only* a court that has this power.

10.3 Licence distribution

The N.R.A., in addition to issuing licences from its own offices, appoints agents to act as licence distributors. These are widely spread throughout each region of the Authority and include fishing tackle retailers, shops, post offices and hotels. Where the Authority runs fisheries on its own reservoirs, licences can usually be purchased on site.

To assist anglers intending to visit an area the Authority issues a number of Regional Angling Guides which give (amongst other goodies) the names and addresses of licence distributors.

10.4 Information given on a licence

Until there is a uniform format of licences issued by the Authority, the wording and layout of those now in existence vary considerably between regions. However, the information each contains is fairly standard and includes the following:

(a) The name of the Authority and the region area to which it applies;
(b) The words "Fishing Licence" and the year;
(c) A reference to the 1975 Act and any other Act, the provisions of which the angler is subject to;
(d) The duration of the licence and the date of expiry;
(e) A serial number;
(f) A statement that the person named is licensed to fish with a rod and line;
(g) The species of fish covered by the licence;
(h) The name and address of the holder;
(i) The date and time of issue; and

(j) The name of the issuing agent.

It may also have extracts from the local byelaws which include details of close seasons, minimum size limits, etc.

10.5 Duration of licences

Licences are issued for varying periods of time – the shortest being for one day and the longest for a year.

Under the old water authorities, the duration of licences of the same description could vary between areas. In some a day licence was valid for a period of twenty four hours whereas in another it expired at midnight on the day on which it was issued. Similarly, a weekly licence could remain valid for 168 hours in one area or expire at midnight on the sixth day after issue in another.

Another example of some of the difficulties that were experienced occurred over the "season licence". In some areas the licence expired at the end of the calendar year which meant that if an angler fished for coarse fish through the winter until the end of the freshwater fishing season on 14 March his licence expired on 31 December and on 1 January he required a new licence to cover him for the rest of the season (and the rest of the calendar year). This could be overcome by making the period of the licence coincide with the financial year and expire on the 31 March – but the same difficulty then arose over salmon and trout season licences where the season started before the end of the financial year. These difficulties could be resolved by standardising licences.

10.6 Areas covered by licences

A licence may cover the whole of an N.R.A. region or a district (or river catchment) within a region and would only be valid for the specified area. For example, if an angler holds a licence to fish for trout in a specified area he will require a second licence if he wants to fish in another area to which his first licence does not apply.

10.7 Species covered by licences

In addition to licences being issued for different periods they
are also issued in respect of the species of fish the angler intends
to fish for.

Three categories of fish are recognised for licensing purposes
i.e. salmon, trout and freshwater fish but this does not mean
that an angler who wants to fish for all species needs to have
three licences. A licence to fish for freshwater fish covers the
angler for the taking of coarse fish and eels; a licence to fish for
trout covers the angler for trout, coarse fish and eels; and a licence
to fish for salmon covers the angler for all species of fish.

The difference in cost of the three categories of licence reflects
the costs of supervising and maintaining the fisheries with which
each category is associated.

The period of use and the area for which it is valid as well
as the species covered are reflected in the cost of a licence.

10.8 Concessionary licences

There are concessionary rates on many types of licence for children
and old age pensioners.

Children under the age of 10 are deemed to be below the age
of ordinary criminal liability and it is therefore impossible to
enforce the requirement for them to have a licence; however most
young anglers regard a fishing licence as an essential part of
their equipment and insist on having one! In some areas there
is a special rate for these younger children.

A child over the age of 10 but below an age determined by
the Authority – usually his sixteenth birthday – needs a licence
which is issued at a concessionary rate. A licence distributor is
within his rights to demand proof of the age of anyone applying
for a concessionary licence if he has doubts about how old that
person is.

The concessions given to old age pensioners may be extended
to seriously disabled persons, especially on reservoirs where the
price of a permit includes a licence element.

10.9 General Licences

If a person has the exclusive right of fishery on a water he can, subject to agreement with the N.R.A. be issued with a "general licence" to cover that fishery. This does away with the need for anyone fishing the water to have an individual licence – provided that he has the written consent of the licencee to be on the fishery. This requirement is essential as it provides proof that the individual is covered by a licence.

The general licence only applies to a particular fishery and if an angler fishes elsewhere (e.g. on the adjoining fishery) he will lose its protection.

The fee charged for such a licence will usually be based upon the licence income that the Authority would expect from those fishing the water if no general licence was issued.

10.10 Block licences

Rather than require each individual angler in a fishing party, such as a club visiting a specific fishery for one day, to take out his own licence, arrangements can usually be made for all involved to be covered by one document – provided sufficient advance notice is given for the licence to be prepared and issued.

The application for the licence should be sent to the local N.R.A. office giving details of all those who will be fishing and enclosing the appropriate fee. The person making the application will then be issued with the licence and will be responsible for producing it to a bailiff if asked to do so. Only those persons named in the licence will be entitled to fish under it.

For certain classes of people, such as the handicapped, a special rate may be agreed by the authority.

10.11 The number of rods covered by a licence

As a general rule a rod licence entitles the holder to use one rod at a time – but there is nothing to prevent him from having several rods with him, provided only one at a time is being used.

In some areas two rods are allowed to be used under one licence for certain types of fish and where this occurs the information is given on the licence.

The purchase of a second rod licence does not automatically allow an angler to use two rods as the use of more than one may be prohibited under byelaw. Reference to the local byelaws will clarify the position.

10.12 The use of hand lines

A normal rod licence to fish does not cover the use of a hand line. Unless expressly permitted under byelaw, when a separate licence would probably apply, the use of a hand line is illegal (except in fishing for sea fish).

10.13 Licences in tidal waters

Although there is a public right of fishery in tidal waters an angler who fishes for or takes any eels, coarse fish, trout or salmon in those waters will require the appropriate licence to do so. The reason for this is that the powers of the N.R.A. under the 1975 Act extend out to the six-mile limit.

No licence is required for fishing for sea fish.

On some rivers the tidal influence extends for many miles inland, providing excellent fishing for both coarse and game fish, as well as for certain species of sea fish e.g. mullet, flounder, shad etc., in water which ranges from fresh to fully saline. The need to have the appropriate licence in these circumstances is often overlooked, particularly by anglers fishing for eels which are classified with freshwater fish for licensing purposes.

Conger eels are sea fish and as such do not come under the Act, but the common eel which is found in both fresh and salt water does. Fortunately, the strict letter of the law is not pursued in cases where eels are taken in the sea but when found in the company of coarse fish in estuarine waters a licence is required.

An angler fishing in the tidal part of a river for mullet may well catch other species for which a licence is required. Because of the similarity of method and tackle used he must be careful not to fall foul of the Act if he is unaware of its provisions or does not hold the appropriate licence.

10.14 Failing to produce a licence

Under section 35 of the 1975 Act a person holding a fishing licence must produce it to a water bailiff if he demands to see it. If the licence is not produced, even though the angler has one but has left it at home, an offence has been committed but, if the angler can satisfy the bailiff that he has a licence and can provide proof of his identity, no action will be taken if the licence is sent to the local N.R.A. office within seven days.

Water bailiffs carry forms on which the angler's name and address, details of the incident and the licence he claims to have are recorded. It also informs him of the procedure to be followed for the production of the licence. The form is completed in duplicate with one copy being given to the angler who is usually required to sign the other acknowledging its receipt.

A licence which is received on time and which was valid at the time of the incident will be returned to the angler.

If the licence is not received within the required period or if it is found to have been invalid at the time of the incident e.g. by being out of date, the angler would find himself liable to prosecution.

10.15 A lost licence

If a licence is lost the holder should notify the Authority immediately in writing giving, if possible, details of its serial number, the species of fish it covered, the approximate date when it was purchased, the name of the distributor from whom it was purchased, and how it came to be lost. If a replacement is issued a small charge may be made.

It is always worth making a separate note of the licence details when it is purchased in case it should be mislaid later.

10.16 Licence inspection by an angler

An angler who produces a fishing licence which is valid at the time and in the place can demand to see the licence of another angler who is fishing. Furthermore, if no licence is produced he can demand the name and address of the other person. If any one fails to comply with this he has committed an offence and should be reported as soon as possible to a bailiff or the Authority. Under section 35 of the 1975 Act anyone guilty of this offence is liable to a heavy fine.

If an angler suspects that another is fishing without a permit, he can ascertain his name and address by demanding to see the licence – assuming that the suspect has a licence.

10.17 Fraudulent use of a licence

As a licence remains the exclusive property of the holder and cannot be transferred, it becomes invalid if used by anyone else. Thus if a person finds a fishing licence and tries to pass it off as his own by using it to fish he would be guilty of a number of offences, including theft by finding, fraud and fishing without a licence.

10.18 Fishing without a licence

Most anglers in preparing for a fishing trip to a strange location go to great lengths to find out in advance about the water, species of fish, bait and tackle they will need, and the permits and licences that they will require. A small number forget the last item until they arrive in the area only to find that the shops are shut. If they risk fishing without a licence and are caught they will get little sympathy from the Authority or the courts – both of whom have heard the excuse that "the shops were shut" all too frequently.

It is incumbent upon an angler to purchase a licence *before* starting to fish. Section 27 of the 1975 Act makes it an offence for any one to use a rod and line for fishing unless licensed to do so to use a rod and line otherwise than in accordance with the conditions of a licence.

Section 27 of the Act reads as follows:

"Section 27 (Unlicensed fishing)
A person is guilty of an offence if in any place in which fishing for fish of any description is regulated by a system of licensing
he
(a) fishes for or takes fish of that description, otherwise than by an instrument he is entitled to use by virtue of a licence,
or otherwise than in accordance with the conditions of the licence, or
(b) has in his possession with intent to use it for that purpose, an instrument other than one which he is authorised to use for that purpose by virtue of such a licence."

The maximum penalty for angling without a licence is £1000.

10.19 Returns of fish caught

Under the Water Act 1989, Schedule 3 of the 1975 Act has been amended to include the need for returns in respect of freshwater fish and eels to be submitted by anglers. Paragraph 32 of the Schedule now reads;-

"Requiring persons to send to the National Rivers Authority returns, in such form, giving such particulars and at such times as may be specified in the byelaws, of the period or periods during which they fished for salmon, trout, freshwater fish or eels, of whether they have taken any and, if they have, of what they have taken."

This means in effect that should the Authority enforce it to the full, every angler to whom a licence is issued would be under a legal obligation to report details of every fish that he caught to the Authority, irrespective of what he was fishing for.

Furthermore it also gives the N.R.A. powers to require anglers to submit details of the actual time they spend fishing.

Chapter 11

CLOSE SEASONS

11.1 The need for close seasons

Dependant upon species, fish, like most animals, breed during certain well defined periods of the year when behavioural and physiological changes render them vulnerable to disease, predation and interference.

Man can do little to prevent disease or predation but he does have the means whereby interference, in terms of human activity, can be curtailed. This is achieved, in part, by the imposition of close seasons, corresponding to periods of greatest spawning activity, when all fishing is prohibited.

The timing of the close seasons can vary according to species but even for the same species these may not be uniform throughout the country.

11.2 Statutory close seasons

There are certain periods in the year during which the majority of a species of fish will spawn (the core time) and these are used to determine the statutory close seasons, i.e. those laid down in the Act, which apply generally unless varied by byelaw. They also take into account the effect which different methods of fishing can have upon the potential spawning stock, but as far as the angler is concerned the following statutory close seasons apply:-

(a) for freshwater (coarse) fish the period between 14 March and 16 June following (when fishing for eels with rod and line is also prohibited);
(b) for trout, other than rainbow trout, the period between 30 September and 1 March following; and
(c) for salmon the period between 31 October and 1 February following.

These are laid down in Schedule 1 of the 1975 Act.

It is an offence to fish during the close seasons, as stated below:-

"Section 19 (2)&(4) (Rod close seasons for salmon and trout)
Any person who fishes for, takes, kills or attempts to take or
kill salmon or trout (other than rainbow trout) with a rod and
line during the annual close season for rod and line shall be
guilty of an offence.

Section 19 (5)
A person shall not be guilty of an offence under the above
in respect of any act done for the purpose of artificial
propagation or a scientific purpose and also,in the case of trout,
for stocking or restocking waters with the previous permission
in writing of the Authority.

*Section 19 (6)&(7) (Rod close season for freshwater fish, eels and
rainbow trout)*
Any person who during the annual close season for freshwater
fish (or rainbow trout) fishes for, takes, kills or attempts to
take or kill any freshwater fish (or rainbow trout) or fishes
for eels by means of a rod and line in any inland waters shall
be guilty of an offence."

11.3 Variations of the close seasons

Although the majority of fish in the country spawn during the
core period there are many exceptions which the Act takes into
account by providing for the seasons to be altered under byelaw
to meet local conditions. These can arise due to the topography
of the area, rainfall, average temperatures, and to some extent
local behavioural or genetic differences in the fish populations.

Where the close seasons are established under byelaw they
replace the statutory ones - but have exactly the same standing
under the law.

The dates between which these byelaws operate can start earlier
or finish later than the statutory ones, but the duration of the
close season must not be less than the minimum laid down in
Schedule 1 of the Act, which is, in respect of rod and line fishing:

(a) for freshwater fish - 93 days;
(b) for trout (excluding rainbow trout) - 153 days; and
(c) for salmon - 92 days.

While there is no statutory close season for rainbow trout, the
Authority can impose its own local close season by means of a
byelaw: this must not be less than 93 days.

It should be noted that the Act defines "freshwater fish" as "fish living in fresh water exclusive of salmon and trout and of any kind of fish which migrate to and from tidal waters and of eels".

11.4 Fishing in the close season

Although section 19 prohibits fishing during the annual close seasons, whether statutory or established under byelaw, under sub-section (8) it also allows fishing to take place during these periods provided certain conditions are observed. These are set out as follows:

"Section 19 (8)
Sub-sections (6) and (7) above do not apply to:
(a) the removal by an owner or occupier, from any several (private) fishery where salmon or trout are specially preserved, of any eels, freshwater fish or rainbow trout not so preserved;
(b) any person fishing with rod and line in any such fishery with the permission in writing of its owner or occupier.
(c) any person fishing with rod and line for eels in any waters in which such fishing is authorised by a byelaw;
(d) the taking of freshwater fish or rainbow trout for a scientific purpose;
(e) the taking of freshwater fish for bait -
(i) in a several fishery with the permission in writing of its owner or occupier, or
(ii) in any other fishery, unless the taking would contravene a byelaw."

Under (a) above the fishery must be *specially preserved as a salmon or trout fishery* in which case the game fishery owner or tenant can improve his fishery by removing unwanted species during this period.

Under (b) he can delegate this power to anglers and can give permission *in writing* for anyone to fish for freshwater fish or eels, which are not so preserved , but, it will be noted, they are not required to remove any fish caught and can return them to the water. The term "specially preserved" in (a) also applies here, which suggests that in a mixed fishery, where freshwater fish are considered to be as of equal importance as game fish, an owner or tenant might find it difficult to justify his giving permission to fish for coarse fish in the close season or to sustain the argument that the fishery was so "specially preserved".

During the close season for freshwater fish they may be taken for bait from a private fishery, with the written permission of the owner or tenant.

The subject of a close season for freshwater fish is an emotive one leading to great deal of debate amongst anglers and fishery managers. One view is that all species need protecting during the spawning period: the opposing one is that, as most fish which are caught are returned to the water, there is no need to protect them. The arguments will, no doubt, continue.

11.5 The close season for rainbow trout

Rainbow trout were introduced into this country about a century ago yet during this time, with a few exceptions, they have never really become naturalised in rivers and lakes but are mainly dependant upon artificial rearing and stocking to maintain their numbers – they do not, therefore, need the protection of a statutory close season.

A close season can, however, be set under byelaw especially in waters which they share with native brown trout where the season is imposed as much in the interests of protecting the brown trout as those of the rainbows, by preventing anglers catching the former under the guise of fishing for the latter. Should the species become naturalised and part of the fauna of this country it is possible that a statutory close season could be imposed at some future time.

11.6 Eels

Eels arrive in this country as elvers, a few inches long, after a journey of two or three years across the Atlantic from the Sargasso Sea (an area of the Atlantic Ocean between the Azores and the West Indies) where they were born. They do virtually all their growing, reaching a weight of several pounds, in our rivers and ponds during the time they spend here, which could be several years, before returning to the ocean once more to breed. It is during this journey that they become sexually mature and, therefore, do not need the protection of a close season.

The Act prohibits fishing for them with a rod and line during the freshwater fish close season, mainly to give protection to freshwater species which can be affected by the activities of eel fishermen – but the exceptions which apply to freshwater fish also apply to eels.

11.7 Lampreys

Of the three species of lamprey found in Britain, i.e. the sea lamprey, the river lamprey and the brook lamprey, the first two species migrate from the sea to spawn in the rivers and, therefore, are not caught by the definition of "freshwater fish" in the Act (See 11.3 above). At one time lampreys were heavily fished for food and are even thought to have brought about the demise of one of our earlier kings through "a surfeit of lampreys"!

The brook lamprey falls within the definition of a freshwater fish as it is non-migratory and therefore is subject to the close season.

It is highly improbable that anyone would wish to fish for these with a rod and line because of their small size and lack of sporting quality.

11.8 Mini-species

The so-called mini-species e.g. minnows, bull heads, loaches, ruffe, sticklebacks and (possibly) gudgeon, although of little sporting value, come within the definition of freshwater fish and are therefore subject to the close season and licensing requirements.

The enforcement of the provisions of the Act in the case of some of the mini-species is rarely applied except where it can be shown that the angler was using the excuse that he was fishing for them as a cover for other activities!

11.9 Accidental taking of fish in the close season

Because the close seasons of some species overlap, e.g. the close season for freshwater fish falls within the fishing season for salmon and trout, and vice versa, it is almost inevitable that an angler fishing for one species will, at some time, accidentally catch another species which is "out of season".

Under section 19 the word "takes" implies "catching" so that a strict interpretation of the Act suggests that the mere catching of a fish which is out of season is an offence. In section 2 of the Act there is a proviso that takes into account the accidental catching of undersized and unclean fish, which would otherwise be illegal: this states that it:

"...does not apply to any person who takes a fish accidentally and returns it to the water with the least possible injury."

No such proviso appears under section 19 but provided that the angler acts in a sensible manner and follows the guidance of section 2, it is most unlikely that any action would be taken against him.

The excuse that a fish caught out of season was kept because it was "deeply hooked and had to be killed to get the hook out" would be unlikely to be accepted by a bailiff or a court. It is far better to sacrifice the hook by cutting the cast and releasing the fish back into the water with the hook still in it – most fish will survive this treatment. One has to weigh up the difference between a hook worth a few pence and a heavy fine.

11.10 Penalties for fishing in the close season

Anyone who fishes during its close season for any species of fish, other than under the exceptions described above would commit an offence under section 19 of the 1975 Act (and any byelaw which amended it) and would, if prosecuted and convicted, be liable to a maximum fine of £1000.

Chapter 12

PROHIBITED METHODS OF FISHING

12.1 Methods prohibited under the Act

If there were no restrictions on the ways in which fish could be caught many species, particularly salmon and trout, would probably be extinct or at least endangered.

Historically, certain instruments, such as gaffs and spears, helped provide impoverished rural families with a supply of fish, especially in the autumn and winter when the fish could be easily caught, but in the last century the dangers associated with their abuse were recognised and they were banned. This is continued under the present legislation.

Section 1 of the 1975 Act states:

"Section 1 (1)(a) and (b) (Prohibited implements)

No person shall use for taking, or have in his possession with intent to take or kill, salmon, trout or freshwater fish

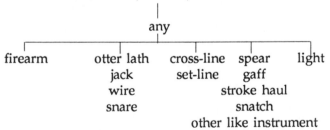

		any		
firearm	otter lath	cross-line	spear	light
	jack	set-line	gaff	
	wire		stroke haul	
	snare		snatch	
			other like instrument	

Section 1 (2)
If any person contravenes this section he shall be guilty of an offence unless he proves to the satisfaction of the court that the act was done for the purpose of the preservation or development of a private fishery with the written permission of the Authority."

Section 2 extends the prohibitions to the use of fish roe as bait. In addition other methods or baits may be banned under byelaw.

It may not be obvious at first sight how some of the listed prohibited implements relate to angling but a closer examination of some of them will reveal a remarkable similarity to tackle and other equipment used in standard angling practice. What prohibits one yet permits the other is the method and intention of its use.

Anglers also can inadvertently break the law by using conventional tackle in an unconventional way.

12.2 The gaff

An *unbarbed* gaff used as an ancillary to angling is an accepted way of landing a hooked fish, but *if the gaff is used in another way, or if it has a barbed hook, it becomes a prohibited implement.*

Even an unbarbed gaff used in angling can be illegal if it is used by one person to land a fish for another (see "Ancillary Use", page 70); or if its use at certain times is prohibited by byelaw to protect fish which are about to spawn or have spawned.

12.3 The tailer

A snare is a wire noose fastened to a stick. This is a much favoured poachers instrument in some areas where the pools in a river are stoned and the fish driven to hide under the river bank, or roots of trees – often with the tail or part of the body exposed. Here the noose is gently lowered into the water and passed around the exposed part of the fish, tightened and the fish is lifted from the water. It is, of course, a prohibited instrument.

A tailer, which is an adaptation of this, is an accepted method of helping an angler land a hooked fish from the water as it serves the same purpose as a gaff without damaging the fish.

What makes the tailer legitimate is its use as an ancillary to angling – if used for any other purpose it becomes illegal.

12.4 Landing net

Although not listed as a prohibited implement a landing net could be regarded as an unlicensed instrument – and therefore illegal – if used to take a fish other than one hooked on rod and line.

12.5 Ancillary use

The use of a gaff, tailer and landing net as an ancillary to angling is provided for under section 1(4) of the Act which states;

"Section 1 (4)
This section shall not apply to any person using or having in his possession with intent to use an unbarbed gaff or tailer as an auxiliary to angling with rod and line."

If this is read in conjunction with section 25(4) which states:

"Section 25 (4)
A fishing licence for the use of a rod and line shall entitle the licensee to use as ancillary to that use a gaff consisting of a plain metal hook without a barb, or a tailer or landing net."

It becomes apparent that only the licensee can use one of these to land a fish he has hooked.

If another person does it for him, even if that person holds a licence himself, a technical offence has been committed.

12.6 Foul hooking

The use of a "stroke-haul" and "snatch" is prohibited under section 1. This consists of one of more treble hooks fastened to the end of a line with a weight attached either just above them or below.

The method of operation is for the implement to be cast into a pool known to contain large numbers of fish: it is then recovered by a series of sharp jerks in the hope that one of the hooks will impale itself in the body of one of the fish thus enabling it to be pulled from the water. The line can be held in the hand or used in conjunction with a rod and reel – in which case the action would not be classed as angling.

The illegal implement is easily recognised but an equally effective method involves conventional fishing lures such as devon minnows or spoon baits, which an unscrupulous angler can use in a similar way. Sometimes fish are foul-hooked unintentionally but provided that they are released back into the water no action would be taken.

If an angler who keeps a foul hooked fish uses the excuse that he took it accidentally, he may well find that this eventuality is covered by a byelaw which makes it an offence *not to return* to the water any fish caught other than by means of a bait or lure taken in the mouth. This is often easier to prove in court and carries a maximum penalty of £1000 – which is considerably less than the penalty under the main body of the Act!

12.7 Other prohibited implements

Section 1 also prohibits other implements which a genuine angler would be unlikely to resort to deliberately, but which he might inadvertently use in his ignorance.

A favourite, used by small boys and poachers, is the "set-line" which is defined as "a fishing line left in water and having attached to it one or more lures or hooks". The common term is probably "night-line" or "bank-line".

It should also be noted that this definition can apply to *a rod and line which is left unattended.*

Also banned is the "otter board" defined as:

"...board, stick or other instrument, whether used with a hand line, or as auxiliary to a rod and line, or otherwise for the purpose of running out lures, artificial or otherwise."

Anything attached to the end of an angler's cast, to help run out his line, in such a way that his bait or lure lies between it and the rod, can be construed as an otter board. A bubble float used this way could be considered to be illegal.

The use of a light to take fish is illegal under this section but if an angler used a torch at night to set up his tackle or to bait his hook it is not likely that any offence would be committed.

12.8 Penalties under section 1

The Act considers any infringement of section 1, which covers all those implements discussed above, to be more serious than offences under many other sections.

A person found guilty by a magistrates' court of an offence under this section would be subject to a maximum fine of £2000, a three month prison sentence or both.

The more serious cases can be sent to the Crown Court, either for trial or for sentence, where the maximum penalty is increased to an unlimited fine, two years in prison or both.

The penalty for an offence committed under byelaw is a maximum of £1000.

To avoid these penalties make sure you know your law!

12.9 The use of fish roe

Section 2 of the Act prohibits the use of any fish roe for the purpose of fishing for salmon, trout or freshwater fish; furthermore, it makes it illegal to buy, sell or have in one's possession any roe of salmon or trout for the same purpose.

The section states:

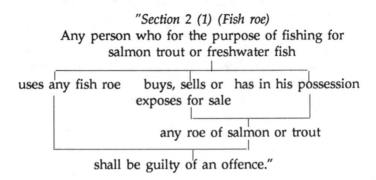

"*Section 2 (1) (Fish roe)*
Any person who for the purpose of fishing for
salmon trout or freshwater fish

uses any fish roe   buys, sells or   has in his possession
                       exposes for sale

any roe of salmon or trout

shall be guilty of an offence."

The term "any fish roe" includes the roe of all game fish, freshwater fish and sea fish.

Salmon or trout roe which has been treated in a special way (often by a secret and closely guarded recipe) is a highly attractive bait for some species of fish and one which commands a high price on the "black market" – as much as £15 a pound. To be effective the roe has to be collected at or about the spawning time and this usually means taking the fish by illegal methods, and out of season, in the headwaters and tributaries of rivers where they would normally lay their eggs. It is in an attempt to put a stop to this practice that trading in salmon or trout roe has been outlawed.

12.10 Other prohibited baits

Roe is the only bait specifically prohibited under the main body of the Act but under byelaw other baits can be banned at some period of the year, e.g. the use of worms or prawns, in fishing for salmon, at the beginning and end of the season.

Where trout stocks are considered to be in danger of being over-fished spinning for them may be prohibited under byelaw.

The N.R.A. can may also impose a ban under byelaw on the use of specified baits – these could include ground bait, live bait, maggots, cheese, etc. – depending upon the need for some form of control on certain fisheries. If fishing in a strange area, it is advisable to check the byelaws for any local variations from the norm.

In the interests of protecting water fowl and, in particular, swans, Parliament has banned the sale of lead shot weights to anglers and over most of the country this has been reinforced by Authority byelaws making its use illegal.

The necessity for some of the restrictions imposed under byelaw is not always obvious and anglers should ensure that proposed future restrictions are fully evaluated and discussed during the usual period for consultation.

Fishery owners and tenants can make their own rules about the use of bait or method of fishing which, provided they do not contravene the Act or any byelaw, can be enforced by the Theft Act.

For offences committed under section 2, and under byelaws relating to the use of baits, the maximum penalty is £1000.

Chapter 13

UNCLEAN AND IMMATURE FISH

13.1 Protection of unclean and immature fish

Section 2 of the Act makes it an offence to take fish when they are too small or when they are about to, or have spawned. The section states:-

Section 2 (2) (Unclean and immature fish)
Any person who knowingly takes, kills or injures or attempts to take, kill or injure, or who buys, sells,or exposes for sale or has in his possession for sale any salmon, trout or freshwater fish which is unclean or immature shall be guilty of an offence.

13.2 Unclean fish

The Act defines an unclean fish as:

"any fish that is about to spawn, or has recently spawned and has not recovered from spawning"

and makes the taking, killing or injuring or attempting to take, kill or injure any salmon, trout or freshwater fish which is unclean an offence.

The term "unclean" applies to any fish, but in practice it applies principally to salmon and trout and the following paragraphs refer to those species.

As the year progresses both sexes of salmon and trout undergo physiological internal and external changes which become most pronounced at the time of spawning. The female becomes very dark in colour and the belly swells with the developing eggs ("hard roe") while the male takes on a reddish colour, grows a pronounced hook on its lower jaw and develops milt ("soft roe") inside its body.

Fish with hard or soft roe in varying stages of development are caught throughout the season. If the mere presence of roe in the body of a fish was a sign that it was unclean all anglers catching fish would be guilty of committing an offence.

A fish of either sex which is approaching spawning is known as a "gravid" fish – but how does this condition relate to the definition of an unclean fish as "a fish about to spawn" and when does a gravid fish become unclean? The answer lies in a simple test which the angler can carry out as soon as he lands a fish – the fish is held vertically by the head while the abdomen is gently squeezed from behind the gills towards the vent. If eggs or milt run from the vent the fish is very close to spawning and should be returned to the water.

The word "kelt" is used to describe salmon or migratory trout which have recently spawned. These are much thinner than unspawned fish, have ragged fins, an inflamed vent and "maggots" on the gills – shortly after spawning they take on a silvery colour which may cause an inexperienced angler fishing in the spring to mistake one for a fresh fish.

13.3 Immature fish

Section 2 of the Act also makes it an offence to take "immature" fish – often referred to as "undersized" fish.

These are defined as:

> "salmon of less than 12 inches in length, measured from the tip of the snout to the fork or cleft of the tail, and any other fish which is of a length less than that prescribed by byelaw."

The 12 inch limit for salmon is intended to protect the immature fish ("parr") during their early life in the river until they turn silver and migrate to the sea as "smolts" – usually when about 6 inches in length. This is considerably less than the length at which even the smallest salmon will spawn but as salmon do the bulk of their growing when at sea it is only during the parr and smolt stages of their life that protection needs to be given.

The above paragraph has to be read with caution. Male salmon parr can and do become sexually active before they go to sea – so much so that they will join in the spawning activities of a fully mature pair of salmon and shed their milt on the eggs as they are laid. If such a fish was caught by an angler and not returned to the water he could be guilty of taking both an immature and unclean fish.

Salmon parr have similar feeding habits, and bear a superficial resemblance, to brown trout which share the same habitat with them. This can lead to confusion with parr being taken, and kept, by anglers in mistake for brown trout – which is illegal. Any parr which is caught when angling should be unhooked gently and returned to the river immediately.

The minimum size for any other species is determined, in theory, by size at which it will spawn for the first time. This can vary considerably between one river and another, e.g. in river "A", roach may spawn when they are 7 inches long, whereas in river "B" the fish could spawn at 8 inches – the difference is catered for under byelaw which would set different size limits for each river. The theoretical approach, however, does not always appear to have been used and anomalies are found in some places.

13.4 Measurement of fish

The accepted method of gauging the length of a fish, and the way in which its minimum length is determined, is to measure it from the tip of the nose or snout to the *fork* of the tail. In some areas the method is different with the length being measured from the tip of the nose or snout to the end of the tail. The difference between the fork length and the tip length can vary from a few millimetres to several centimetres, depending on the size and species of the fish.

13.5 Accidental catching of unclean or immature fish

Under section 2 of the Act the possibility of a person catching an unclean or immature fish accidentally is recognised and provision is made that no offence is committed if the fish is returned to the water with the "least possible injury".

The section states:-

"Section 2 (3)

Sub-section (2) above does not apply to any person who takes a fish accidentally and returns it to the water with the least possible injury."

The requirement that immature fish be returned to the water with the "least possible injury" could be contravened if the fish were placed in a keep net when their confinement could be construed as causing them injury. In some areas this is permitted under byelaw.

13.6 Immature "bait fish"

The use of immature fish as live or dead bait may be permitted by byelaw – this will depend upon area and local practice. Never attempt to use immature fish for bait unless the byelaws permit (or do not prohibit) it.

13.7 Club and fishery size limits

An angling club, or any fishery, is not constrained by the minimum size limits established under byelaw and can set its own minimum size limits for any species of fish *provided* that the limits are not less than those laid down under an Authority byelaw.

13.8 Penalty for taking unclean or immature fish

The offence can only be tried in a magistrates' court where the maximum penalty that can be awarded is a fine of £1000.

Chapter 14

FISH MOVEMENT AND STOCKING

14.1 The need for controls

If there were no controls over the movement and stocking of fish, enthusiastic, but misguided, individuals could completely change the nature of fisheries by introducing alien species that would displace or inhibit the native fish through competition or predation. Unfortunately, this has already been done on some fisheries.

Such introductions can also lead to a spread of disease or parasites that are endemic, but not necessarily lethal, in the aliens which the native fish have no defence against leading to widespread mortalities.

The 1975 Act takes steps to control stocking and there are further provisions under the Diseases of Fish Acts that can be applied to control disease.

14.2 Legal requirements

Before any inland waters can be stocked the consent of the N.R.A. must be obtained, as required under section 30 of the Act which states:-

"Section 30 (Introduction of fish)
A person shall be guilty of an offence if he introduces any fish or spawn of fish into an inland water or has in his possession any fish or spawn of fish intending to introduce it into an inland water unless he first obtains the written consent of the Authority."

If the right to stock is not contained in the deeds of a fishery the consent of the owner would also be required beforehand.

14.3 Preparing to stock

Preferably any stock fish should be obtained from a reputable fish farm and stocking should only be carried out after a number of logical steps and formalities of both biological and legal importance have been completed. These include the following:-

(a) Survey the fishery to determine if it is suitable for the species of fish it is intended to stock with. (N.B. The water quality of the source from which the fish are coming should be similar to that of the fishery into which they will be stocked. Trout from a fish farm with an alkaline water supply do not do well in a fishery which has an acidic water).

(b) Assess the compatibility of the proposed stock fish with the native species. The Authority is unlikely to give consent to an alien species.

(c) Make certain that the fishery has the capacity to hold and sustain the increased population.

(d) Make preliminary enquiries that the number and species of fish wanted can be supplied and fix a provisional delivery date - but do not place a firm order.

(e) Make arrangements for an alternative source of supply in case the first choice is unable to meet its commitments.

(f) Apply to the Authority for stocking consent, giving information about:-

(i) number and species of fish;
(ii) where they are to be obtained from;
(iii) the location of the fishery they are destined for;
(iv) details of the existing fish population; and
(v) the date of the proposed stocking.

(The Authority may supply a form on which the relevant information can be entered and an advisory leaflet on the subject).

(g) If the consent is granted send a copy of it to the supplier when the order for the fish is placed.

(h) Inform the Authority well in advance of the time when the fish are expected to be delivered.

The consent issued by the Authority to stock any waters (except a fish farm) must be in writing to be valid.

14.4 Alternative sources of stock fish

Whenever possible fish should be obtained from a reputable source, such as a fish farm or hatchery.

Some fisheries periodically remove unwanted fish which are offered for sale. These should only be purchased if the supplier has been cleared by the Authority, or the Ministry, as it is possible that they could carry parasites or bacteria that would infect the fish in their new habitat.

Irrespective of the source, the procedures described above should be followed – in particular the application for consent. The Authority would not allow fish from a suspect source to be introduced into any waters.

14.5 Inter-fishery transfer of fish

The transfer of fish by a fishery owner or occupier (or club) from one fishery in his ownership to another is treated in exactly the same way as any other stocking and requires Authority consent; it is illegal if no consent is granted.

Similarly, the practice (fortunately now dying out) whereby an angler catching a specimen fish in one water transports it back to his home fishery is also illegal unless consent has been granted – this applies whether the number of fish is just one or many.

Anyone who is granted consent to capture fish in one location and move them to another will also need to seek an additional consent to use the instrument or method intended. If the intended method is either electrical fishing, explosives or poisons, consent under section 5 of the Act will be required as these methods are otherwise illegal (consent to use poisons also has to be approved by the Ministry). Other methods not covered by section 5, such as netting, may be prohibited under byelaw unless consent for their use has been given.

If the fish to be moved are salmon or trout, any method used needs to be authorised and licensed under section 25, for which a fee may be payable.

14.6 Use of live-bait

The use of live-bait is a form of temporary stocking – provided that the fish does not escape off the hook, or escapes being taken by a predator and is later removed from the fishery. However, even the shortest of time spent in the water is sufficient for it to pass any harmful bacteria or parasites that it carries into the environment.

For this reason, where the use of live-bait is permitted there are usually strict rules relating to its original source and disposal at the end of fishing. These can include the requirement that only live-bait caught in the water being fished can be used and that all unused fish must be returned to the water from whence they originated.

In other areas the use of live-bait is totally prohibited and this may extend to dead bait coming from waters affected by disease or parasites.

The byelaws relating to live-bait vary between areas and the angler should check the local byelaws before starting to fish.

14.7 Stocking and fish movement by the N.R.A.

Under the various statutes under which it operates the Authority has a number of duties which include the duty to:

"maintain, improve and develop the salmon fisheries, trout fisheries, freshwater fisheries and eel fisheries in the area for which it exercises functions under the Act."

This enables it to do many things which are denied to the individual, except with its consent, including moving fish and stocking.

This apparent omnipotence is tempered by the fact that, like any individual, the Authority is required to comply with the common law (unless this has been over ridden by statute for certain functions) and statute law, including the Theft Act, e.g. it cannot remove any fish or the eggs of fish from a private fishery without the permission of the owner or occupier.

14.8 Ministerial control of fish movements

There are strict controls, operated by M.A.F.F., over the importation of live fish and the eggs of certain species under the Diseases of Fish Acts of 1937 and 1983. Despite this, loopholes have been discovered which lets some species of cold water fish escape the net by being imported under the guise of "ornamental" fish which are not covered by the Acts. It is alleged that Spring Vireamia in Carp (SVC) entered the country in this way. Concern has been expressed that this situation could get worse when trade restrictions between countries of the E.E.C. are abandoned in 1992.

Not all disease comes from overseas; there are many which are endemic in this country.

Some fish diseases, if uncontrolled, can have a catastrophic effect upon fish populations. Certain of them are notifiable and any suspect outbreak must be reported immediately to the Ministry which then investigates it. If the disease is confirmed the Minister can make an order prohibiting the movement of fish from a location or area in which the disease is present. In the case of a nationwide outbreak, such as the UDN epidemic of the late '60s and '70s, virtually all the country can be subject to restrictions.

If disease breaks out in a fish farm the Ministry imposes a ban on fish movement to and from it, then monitors the situation until a clean bill of health can be given. The ban could last for several months if the outbreak is severe.

14.9 Fish used in biological control

Some species of exotic fish if released into the wild in this country may be beneficial to the environment. A case in point is the grass carp, a herbivore which originates in eastern Europe and the Far East, that can be used to control weed growth.

However, these fish were not introduced in a haphazard manner but were subject to a decade of assessment and investigation by the Ministry of Agriculture, Fisheries and Food to determine if they would threaten native stocks and how effective they would be in carrying out the task they were intended for.

Although these fish are now available to the general public they should only be imported into this country under licence and are subject to Authority approval before they can be introduced to any waters.

Chapter 15

SALE OF SALMON AND TROUT

15.1 The need for restrictions

The need for restricting the sale of both salmon and trout to certain times of the year is to prevent the over-exploitation of species, which are a valuable food source, during the period when they are at their most vulnerable, i.e. at the approach to and during their spawning season.

Species which are not in demand as food and which are not vulnerable at the present time fall outside this requirement.

15.2 The legal position

Provisions relating to the sale of fish, contained in section 22 of the 1975 Act only apply to salmon and trout. There is no prohibition on the sale of rainbow trout or freshwater fish.

The period when sale is prohibited is:-

(a) for salmon between 31 August and the following 1 February, and

(b) trout between 31 August and the following 1 March.

(There are exceptions to these dates which are discussed below.)

The relevant wording of the section is:-

"Section 22 (1) (Sale of salmon and trout)
Any person who buys, sells, or exposes for sale or has in possession for sale any salmon between 31 August and the following 1 February;

or

any trout (other than rainbow trout) between 31 August and the following 1 March shall be guilty of an offence."

15.3 Freshwater fish

Freshwater fish are not covered by this section because at the present time their numbers are not threatened by a demand for them as food. If, at some future time, a particular species, e.g. roach, became a gastronomic delicacy (it is possible!) and its numbers were threatened in order to satisfy the demands of gourmets it is probable that a restriction on its sale would be imposed.

15.4 Rainbow trout

Rainbow trout are not covered by this section of the Act for two main reasons:-

(a) as an introduced species which has not established itself in the fisheries of this country, but has to be sustained by artificial means, there is no need to protect them during a spawning season; and

(b) as a species it forms the backbone of this country's food-fish rearing industry, and any restriction on its sale would seriously hamper these commercial operations.

15.5 Exceptions to the restrictions on sale

The provisions of section 22 (1) above are general and apply in particular to fish caught commercially – but these do not apply to the sale of fish if imported, frozen or caught outside the United Kingdom. Also any salmon or trout (other than unclean or immature fish) caught within the United Kingdom by any net, instrument or device can be sold if its capture was lawful at the time and in the place where they were caught.

This means that an angler who catches a salmon, which is not unclean, towards the end of the season – which may end several weeks after the 31 August – can sell his catch. The section goes on to state:-

"Section 22 (2)

Sub-section (1) above shall not apply to any person buying, selling or exposing for sale, or having in his possession for sale, any salmon or trout (other than unclean or immature salmon or trout) caught within the United Kingdom if its capture by any net, instrument or device was lawful at the time and place where it was caught."

15.6 Sale of fish for stocking

There is a further exception under this section which applies to the sale of trout which is permitted for stocking and certain other purposes. In covering this the section states:-

> "*Section* 22 (3)
> A person shall not be guilty of an offence in respect of trout under this section for any act done for the purpose of artificial propagation of fish or the stocking or restocking of waters or for some scientific purpose."

15.7 Onus of proof

Under section 22 the burden of proving that no offence had been committed in respect of any salmon or trout bought, sold, exposed for sale or in possession of a person for sale between the relevant dates, lies with the person buying, selling, exposing for sale or in possession for sale of any such fish.

15.8 Penalty for offences under section 22

If found guilty of an offence under this section, a maximum fine of £1000 could be imposed.

Chapter 16

DEALING IN AND HANDLING SALMON

16.1 Dealer licensing

Until the passing of the Salmon Act 1986 there were no restrictions on the buying and selling of salmon – apart from those relating to times of sale (see Chapter 15) – a fact which certain persons seized upon to create a lucrative trade in illegally caught fish. The magnitude of this illicit operation has never been fully assessed but the numbers of fish involved are thought to at least equal the reported catches by legitimate methods.

Section 31 of the 1986 Act went some way towards resolving this by making provision for the Minister, if he so wished, to make an Order under which it would be an offence for anyone to deal in fresh, chilled or frozen salmon, unless he has a dealer's licence.

To give effect to this the Minister issued a consultation paper in which the proposals were set out and which attracted responses from a wide range of interests. Some were of the opinion that the proposals did not go far enough by exempting hotels, restaurants and retailers from the need to be licensed which would leave loopholes that could be exploited. Others offered outright opposition to the scheme.

After deliberating on the views submitted and consulting with many of the interests the Minister announced in February 1990 that:

"The Government has considered most thoroughly these responses as well as the benefits – in relation to the costs and other burdens involved – which these schemes might bring to the continuing efforts to combat poaching...Many who favoured salmon dealer licensing in principle argued that the schemes would not be effective with the range of exemptions that we proposed. Some interests felt that salmon dealer licensing would work effectively only if compulsory carcass tagging (for which there is no present legislative provision) was also introduced. On the other hand, fish farmers and many fish traders took the view that the schemes, even with the proposed exemptions, imposed an excessive and inappropriate regulatory burden on trade in legally obtained, and particularly farmed or imported, fish.

The Government recognises that the proposed exemptions could undermine the potential effectiveness of the scheme...It became clear that the proposed scheme would impose a heavy burden on many businesses even with the proposals for exemptions and record keeping requirements kept to a minimum. For many traders and markets the record keeping requirements, in particular, would pose virtually insurmountable difficulties. *Accordingly, it has now been decided not to proceed further with the schemes for licensing of dealers."*

This decision will be a disappointment to many as it will have the effect of leaving open a very wide door for the disposal of illegally caught fish.

However, the provision remains in the Act and it is to be hoped that some future Minister with perhaps a more sympathetic attitude towards protecting the salmon will resurrect it.

16.2 Fish suspected of being illegally caught

Although one way of controlling the sale of fish illegally caught has now been vetoed by the Minister this is off-set to some extent by section 32 of the Salmon Act 1986 which deals with handling salmon in suspicious circumstances. This states that;

"A person shall be guilty of an offence if at a time when he believes or it would be reasonable for him to suspect, that a relevant offence has at any time been committed in relation to any salmon he receives the salmon, or undertakes or assists in its retention, removal or disposal by or for the benefit of another person, or if he arranges to do so."

Section 22 of this Act creates a corresponding offence in Scotland of possessing salmon which have been taken illegally and is intended to work in association with, and be complementary to, section 32.

Brown trout, rainbow trout, char and other species of fish are not covered by this section – which seems a pity as there is also quite a lucrative trade in illegally caught trout!

It is important to note the difference between the definition of the term 'salmon' as defined in section 40 of the Act as meaning:-

"all migratory fish of the species Salmo salar and Salmo trutta commonly known as salmon and sea trout respectively or any part of any such fish".

and the definition given in the 1975 Act which defines salmon as:-

"all fish of the salmon species and includes part of a salmon."

N.B. This definition excludes sea trout.

The effect of this section is to make it an offence for anyone to handle salmon, whether for gain or not, who has doubt about its origin.

16.3 "Relevant offence"

A "relevant offence" is an offence committed in England and Wales or Scotland under the law applicable to the place where the salmon was taken, killed or landed. Thus a person in England could be guilty under section 32 if the relevant offence was committed by the taking of a salmon illegally in Scotland – and vice versa.

This is a major breakthrough in combating poaching, as it ignores national boundaries, and overcomes the problems associated with the different legislation and legal codes.

16.4 Ignorance of a relevant offence

For the purpose of section 32, the buyer or handler of the illegally caught fish does not need to believe or have grounds for suspicion that it relates to a specific offence nor exclusively to a relevant offence or offences.

The fact that he suspects, or believes that the fish were taken illegally, is in itself sufficient for him to commit the offence. However, if legal proceedings are taken against him it shall be a defence to show that no relevant offence had in fact been committed in respect of the salmon in question.

16.5 Sea trout

As stated above, for the purposes of the 1986 Act, the term "salmon" includes sea trout. It follows that one can also commit an offence by buying or handling a sea trout if it is suspected that it was taken illegally.

16.6 Preventing handling offences

A person cannot be guilty under this section in relation to a relevant offence. An angler who caught a salmon illegally, e.g. when not licensed to do so, and kept it, would be caught by the relevant offence under section 27 of the 1975 Act only – however, an *alternative* offence under section 32 of the 1986 Act could be levied against him.

Probably the most frequent offence under this section occurs through the sale of salmon to hotels, fishmongers and individuals when the receiver of the fish, believes or it would be reasonable for him to suspect, that the fish had been taken illegally. Suspicion could be aroused by a number of possibilities including fish being offered for sale at the "back door":-

(a) by persons unknown,
(b) which show net or gaff marks, or
(c) at a price well below that of the market,

To avoid being accused under this section anyone offered salmon from any source, other than a bona fide retailer or a known licensed fisherman, should be particularly careful, especially if any of the above possibilities is apparent, and refuse the fish unless the vendor can produce proof of his credentials and satisfy that the fish had been caught legally.

Apart from the water bailiffs who are always on the look-out for offences of this kind, the cooperation of the public can be of immense help and anyone who is offered fish from a doubtful source is invited to report the facts promptly to the N.R.A. giving, if possible, a description of the person and the registration number of any vehicle involved.

To further impress upon the public the dangers of buying illegally caught salmon some regions of the N.R.A. have published a pamphlet explaining the legal position, the things to look for and persons to contact. It also stresses that the temptation to buy cheap salmon could prove expensive!

16.7 Effect upon poaching

It may be some years before the full impact of this section of the Act can be realistically assessed but already a number of successful prosecutions have been brought and heavy penalties imposed.

If section 31 had been implemented, the two sections used together would have helped provide an even more effective deterrent to the disposal of illegally caught fish by closing more of the outlets that now exist.

One surprising thing about the sale of poached salmon is that despite the fact that salmon farming has now reduced the price of fish to a level which all can afford there still remains the mystique and reputation of wild salmon, and people are prepared to buy them at a premium. As demand for these fish outstrips the supply some people are determined to cash-in on the position and catch them by any means. If the sale of poached salmon can be controlled it will reduce the incidence of poaching – the decision rests with the public many of whom, if the truth were really known, rely more upon the price paid than gastronomic appreciation to tell the difference between farmed and wild salmon!

In view of the successful prosecutions already brought it is anticipated that more potential buyers of poached salmon will have second thoughts about doing so bearing in mind that, if they do, they may find it extremely difficult, due to the provisions of the Act, to put up a defence if they are prosecuted.

16.8 Penalties under the 1986 Act

For handling salmon illegally the penalties are;

(a) on summary conviction, imprisonment for not more than three months or a fine not exceeding the statutory maximum (currently £2000), or both; or

(b) on indictment, imprisonment for not more than two years or an unlimited fine, or both.

Chapter 17

BYELAWS

17.1 Byelaw application

Prior to the reorganisation of the water industry under the 1989 Act, each of the water authorities had its own code of fishery byelaws aimed specifically at meeting the local conditions and requirements.

Most of these byelaws are still in operation under the N.R.A. and will probably remain so for some time. Eventually, it is probable that these will be amended or replaced by others to reflect a national approach while still protecting the special needs of each river system.

Some of these byelaws have been discussed earlier in the context of local variations to certain sections in the main body of the Act.

17.2 Making byelaws

In the past each water authority was responsible for determining the need for its own byelaws – this is now the responsibility of the N.R.A. through each of its regions.

When the need to make a byelaw has been established by the Authority, usually in consultation with affected interests, it publishes, in the London Gazette and such other papers as are deemed expedient, details of its proposals and of its intention of applying to the Minister (or the Secretary of State for Wales) for confirmation. It also serves notices on any public authority which will be affected and makes copies of its proposals available for inspection by the public at its offices. Anyone who applies for a copy of the proposals is entitled to receive one free of charge.

The byelaw will not come into being until it has been confirmed by the Minister.

Should there be a number of objections, the Minister may require a public enquiry to be held by an Inspector of his choosing before making a decision. This would give both the objectors and supporters the opportunity of having their views heard.

Depending upon the number of witnesses, the complexity of the evidence and the the time taken for the Inspector to prepare his report, the Minister can give his verdict in as little as a few weeks – on the other hand it has been known for him to take a year or more.

17.3 Purposes for which byelaws can be made

Under section 28 of the Act, byelaws that could affect angling can be made for a number of purposes including:-

(a) fixing or altering the close season for salmon and trout and dispensing with the close season for freshwater fish or rainbow trout;

(b) specifying the dimensions of keep-nets;

(c) prohibiting the use, and time of use, of certain instruments;

(d) prohibiting the taking or removal of any fish whether alive or dead from any waters;

(e) fixing minimum size limits for trout or freshwater fish;

(f) prohibiting or regulating angling above or below any dam or other obstruction;

(g) prohibiting or regulating angling during the hours of darkness;

(h) requiring anglers to submit details of fish caught;

(i) regulating the use of any lure or bait;

(j) determining a time when the use of a gaff shall be lawful;

(k) authorising angling for eels during the close season for freshwater fish and

(l) doing other things for the better execution of the Act and better protection, preservation and improvement of the fisheries.

Some of the above are discussed below with examples of current byelaws, which apply in specified areas. Where appropriate the reasons for which they were originally made, and the name of the predecessor authority which made them, are also given.

17.4 Alteration of the close season

The close season for freshwater fish can be changed from that set out in the Act. Examples of such changes follow:-

(a) The Yorkshire River Authority byelaws amended the close season for freshwater fish which:

"shall be from 28 February to the following 31 May, both dates inclusive";

(b) The North West Water Authority changed the annual close season for brown trout to the,

"period from and including the 1 October to and including the 14 March following".

In both these examples the start and finish date of the close season is given – whereas in the body of the Act a close season is given as the period between "A" and the following "B" with date "A" being the last day of the open season and date "B" as the first day of the next open season. This difference in definition can be confusing and has, in the past, led to anglers breaking the law inadvertently.

(c) The South West Water Authority dispensed with the annual close season for freshwater fish.

(d) Other Authorities dispensed with the close season for rainbow trout under byelaw but this is not necessary as there is no close season under the Act – but one can be imposed under byelaw.

17.5 Keep-nets

To overcome the damage suffered by fish held in keep-nets, due to overcrowding and de-scaling from rough net material (and often considered to be a major factor contributing to fish disease), some water authorities introduced byelaws which set a minimum size limit for keep-nets and encouraged the use of less harmful material such as "micro-mesh". There is no uniform minimum standard size laid down for keep nets at the present but it seems logical that one be established nationally in the not too distant future by the N.R.A.

A North West Water Authority byelaw, still extant, states:

"(i)   No person shall use a keep-net for retaining fish during the annual close season for freshwater fish.

(ii)   No person shall use a keep-net:

(a) of less than 2.0 metres in extended length;

(b) with rings less than 380 mm in diameter or, if rectangular, less than 355 mm by 255 mm;

(c) with wider spacing of rings than one ring per 300 mm, excluding the top ring; and

(d) with a mesh size of more than 16 mm, measured diagonally from knot to knot when stretched and wet.

(iii) The use of keep-nets commonly known as "micro-mesh" nets is permitted. In the case of such nets the width of the mesh measured when wet but un-stretched shall not exceed 8 mm and such nets shall comply with (ii)(a),(b) and (c) above."

17.6 Prohibition on the use of certain instruments

A limit on the number of rods which an angler can use is imposed under some byelaws. A Welsh Water Authority byelaw, for example, states:

"No person shall fish with more than one rod and line at a time for salmon or trout (including rainbow trout) or with more than two rods and lines at a time for freshwater fish and eels."

A South West Water Authority byelaw limits the fishing instruments that may be used. This states:

"No person shall use in fishing for salmon or migratory trout in the Area any instrument other than a net specified in..., a fixed engine lawfully used or a rod and line."

17.7 Removal of fish from any waters

A person who did not hold a fishing licence and/or who had taken a fish illegally could use the excuse that he found it dead in the water. This excuse was prevalent at one time until the water authorities introduced byelaws to counter it. A Welsh Water Authority byelaw, for example, states:

"No person (other than a water bailiff of the Authority acting in his official capacity) shall take or remove any live fish or any dead fish from any waters within the Authority's area, except in accordance with the written authority of the Authority or unless otherwise he is lawfully authorised so to do."

A North West Water Authority byelaw is more succinct:

"No person may take or remove from any waters within the area of the Authority without lawful authority any fish, whether dead or alive."

The need for these byelaws to cover this weakness is common throughout the country. For this reason a similar provision could be included in the main body of any new fishery Act, rather than leaving it to be dealt with at local level under byelaw.

17.8 Size limits

All water authorities introduced byelaws that established minimum size limits for fish. Some only dealt with trout while others covered most species. An example of the latter was the Thames Water Authority whose byelaw stated:

"No person shall take away from any waters within the area any fish of a kind and of a size less than such as is herein after prescribed, that is to say:

Barbel	40cm	Gudgeon	13cm
Bleak	10cm	Perch	22cm
Bream	30cm	Pike	60cm
Carp	30cm	Roach	18cm
Crucian Carp	18cm	Rudd	20cm
Chub	30cm	Tench	25cm
Dace	15cm	Brown trout	25cm
Grayling	25cm		

The size shall be ascertained by measuring from the tip of the snout to the end of the tail fin..."

Other authorities required the measurements to be taken from the "tip of the nose to the fork of the tail". The lack of uniformity in the wording of byelaws can be confusing and lead to an angler unintentionally taking an undersized fish if he is confused over where the measurements should be made.

17.9 Fishing near obstructions

Congregations of fish (especially migratory fish) below weirs make them easy prey for poachers using such things as snatches under the guise of angling.

To prevent this most water authorities made byelaws prohibiting angling within a certain distance above and below a weir or other obstruction, such as a natural waterfall. These could apply generally or relate to a specific location.

A Severn Trent byelaw is an example of the latter, this states:

"No person shall take or attempt to take, by any means, salmon, trout or freshwater fish or eels within a distance of 15 metres above and 45 metres below or downstream of the crest of Shrewsbury Weir."

17.10 Prohibition on angling at night

It has been found necessary in some areas to prohibit angling at night to prevent abuses. An example of a byelaw dealing with this is one made by the Yorkshire Water Authority which states:

"No person shall fish for, take or kill any salmon, trout or freshwater fish with rod and line in the River Esk between the downstream side of Ruswarp Road Bridge and the Whitby harbour mouth between the expiration of the first hour after sunset on any day and the beginning of the last hour before sunrise on the following morning during the months of September and October in any year."

17.11 Anglers' catch returns

Catches, especially of salmon and sea-trout, made by both commercial fishermen and anglers reflect to some degree the abundance of fish in river system. In order that this information can be collected and used most authorities required fishermen to send in details of all fish caught in a season.

A Welsh Water Authority byelaw states:

"Any person fishing for salmon or migratory trout (sea trout) to whom a licence is issued by the Authority shall, immediately upon the expiration of the period of the licence, make a full and true return to the Authority on a form contained on the licence, of the location and of the date on which any salmon or migratory trout were taken and the number and weight of all such salmon or migratory trout taken, or a statement that the person had taken no such fish."

The use of this type of byelaw was used by the Thames Water Authority to check on the presence of zander in its waters and required anglers catching any to:

"make a written return to the Authority of the number and place of capture and shall thereafter give such other particulars as the Authority may reasonably require."

It should be noted that under the provisions of Schedule 17 of the Water Act 1989 anglers may in future be required to submit details of catches of trout, freshwater fish and eels as well as information on the amount of time spent fishing.

17.12 Restrictions on baits and lures

Where it is deemed desirable to restrict or prohibit certain methods of fishing in order to prevent abuse or protect fish stocks byelaws can be introduced for the purpose.

A Severn Trent Water Authority byelaw states

"No person shall:
(a) in fishing with rod and line for salmon in the Severn area use any float in conjunction with any lure or bait; and
(b) in fishing with rod and line during the annual close season for freshwater fish, use any float or bait (including ground bait) other than artificial or natural fly, spinners, minnows of worms."

A Welsh Water Authority byelaw prohibits the use of worm or prawn in fishing for salmon or migratory trout at the start and end of season, and the use of maggots, pupae and non-aquatic larvae is prohibited on most rivers.

17.13 Use of a gaff

To help protect kelts and unclean fish (both of which must be returned uninjured to the water) from injury from anglers gaffs, most water authorities introduced byelaws prohibiting its use at certain times of the year. Although achieving the same objective some byelaws are couched in prohibitive terms while others are permissive.

For example a Northumbrian Water Authority byelaw is prohibitive and states:

"During the months of February, March, April and October in each year no person shall use a gaff in connection with fishing with rod and line in any waters in the area other than landlocked lakes and ponds."

The Wessex Water Authority, on the other hand, has a byelaw which gives the times when a gaff is permitted. This states:

"It shall be lawful to use a gaff in connection with fishing with rod and line for salmon or migratory trout in ..... between the first day after the end of the appropriate close season and the 31st day of August following."

17.14 Close season angling for eels

Although the Act makes angling for eels illegal during the freshwater fish close season, except under the conditions laid down in section 19 (8) (See 11.6), a byelaw can countermand this.

A Severn Trent byelaw does this and states:

"It shall be lawful to fish for eels with rod and line during the annual close season for freshwater fish in the Water Authority Area."

17.15 For the better protection of fisheries

Byelaws of this nature are not directly related to amending any particular section of the Act. They provide a "catch all" for regulating other matters that could be detrimental to fisheries but which are not specifically catered for.

Byelaws, which fall under this heading, include such subjects as:

(a) making it obligatory to return any fish not hooked in the mouth by fair angling;
(b) prohibit the use of lead shot of a certain size;
(c) prohibiting the introduction of any live or dead fish etc. into any waters;
(d) limiting the numbers of fish taken by angling which can be removed from any water; and
(e) controlling local practices.

17.16 Anglers awareness of byelaws

An angler is expected to know the law relating to his sport, including all byelaws. If he is unsure about them before he goes fishing, he should get a copy of the local byelaws from the Authority.

The maximum penalty for a byelaw offence is a fine of £1000.

Chapter 18

ORDERS

18.1 Orders made under the 1975 Act

The difference between a byelaw and an Order is not often clear to the layman.

A byelaw, as has been illustrated above, allows certain elements within a section of the Act to be changed, within prescribed limits while retaining its original intention, to enable it to be applied more effectively at local level – in other words it adapts the Act to meet local conditions.

To become effective a byelaw has to be processed according to the procedure laid down and approved by the Minister or the Secretary of State for Wales.

An Order broadens the provisions of the Act.

Examples of the subjects that can be dealt with under an Order include:

(a) the imposition, collection and recovery of a fishery rate by the Authority assessed on the owners and occupiers of fisheries in all or part of its area,

(b) enabling the Authority with the approval of the Minister to erect and work a fixed engine for catching salmon and migratory trout (this is initially limited to a period of five years but can be extended for further periods, not exceeding five years, by the Minister); and

(c) to modify in relation to the fisheries any of the provisions of the Act which relate to the regulation of fisheries.

An example of an Order modifying fishery regulation can occur where the provisions of section 1 of the 1975 Act, which apply only to salmon, trout and freshwater fish, need to be extended to include eels.

An Order only becomes effective when it has received Parliamentary approval – unlike a byelaw which can be approved by the Minister.

Chapter 19

WATER BAILIFFS AND THEIR POWERS

19.1 The role of water bailiffs

Most anglers have encountered a water bailiff at some time or another – usually when he asks to inspect a fishing licence – but few are fully aware of his role or what his powers are. This section sets out to explain both.

The Water Act 1989 places a duty upon the N.R.A. "to maintain, improve and develop salmon fisheries, trout fisheries, freshwater fisheries and eel fisheries" in England and Wales and makes the N.R.A. responsible for implementing and enforcing its provisions and those of the 1975 Act.

In order to maintain fisheries, and thereby provide a base for their improvement and development, the Acts prohibit and/or restrict practices that would otherwise be detrimental to a fishery resource that is both vulnerable and liable to exploitation.

The provisions of the Acts have to be efficiently policed if they are to serve their purpose and to give effect to this water bailiffs are appointed by the N.R.A. to enforce them. They are helped in this task by specific powers granted to them in the 1975 Act.

A water bailiff has other duties to perform in addition to his policing role but, for the purpose of this book, only this latter role will be examined and discussed.

19.2 The powers of a water bailiff

To assist a water bailiff in carrying out his duties of enforcement sections 31 to 36 of the Act set out in detail the powers that he can use. These are considerable and include the following:-

(a) he can enter onto land to examine any dam, weir, obstruction or artificial water course;

(b) he can examine any instrument or bait that he has reasonable cause to suspect of being used in contravention of the Act or any container suspected of holding such instrument or bait;

(c) he can stop and search any boat or vehicle he suspects of containing any fish caught, or instrument used, in contravention of the Act;

(d) he can seize any fish, instrument, boat, vehicle or anything liable to be forfeited in pursuance of the Act;

(e) he can enter onto land for the purpose of preventing any offence under the Act, except a dwelling house, its curtilage or any lands used exclusively for the preservation of wild fowl;

(f) he can be granted a warrant by a Magistrate to enter any land on or near a river if he has reason to suspect an offence under the Act;

(g) he can be granted a warrant by a Magistrate to search premises suspected of being used in connection with any offence under the Act;

(h) he can arrest anyone fishing illegally at night;

(i) he can demand the name and address, and to see the fishing licence of anyone who is fishing or whom he suspects of being about to fish or of fishing within the last half hour; and

(j) he is deemed to be a constable for the enforcement of the Act or any Order or Byelaw made under it and to have the same powers and privileges and be subject to the same liabilities as a constable by virtue of the common law or any statute.

By virtue of this last item his powers are considerably extended and these will be discussed in context later.

19.3 Proof of appointment

In some areas water bailiffs are recognised by the uniform they wear – but, as yet, these are not general issue throughout the country. Elsewhere the water bailiffs carry out their duties in ordinary clothes and may display an arm band to indicate who they are.

While the dress worn on duty can vary between regions, water bailiffs have one item of identity that is common to all – they each have a warrant of appointment. This is the *only legally acceptable proof that a person is a water bailiff* and if he purports to carry out his duty he should always produce this warrant as proof of his identity and position. Section 36(2) of the Act states:-

"The production by a water bailiff of evidence of his appointment shall be sufficient warrant for him exercising the powers conferred by this Act".

The format of warrants may not be standard but whatever form they take the following information should be included:

(a) the name of the N.R.A. or his local region or both;
(b) reference to the Salmon and Freshwater Fisheries Act 1975 and other statutes from which he derives his powers;
(c) the name of the holder and a declaration that he is a water bailiff appointed under the Act with the powers to implement its provisions; and
(d) the signature of the issuing officer.

Never produce anything for, or give anything to, a person who claims he is a water bailiff unless he produces his warrant and allows you to inspect it.

19.4 Licence inspection by a water bailiff

With few exceptions all persons fishing are required to be in possession of a valid fishing licence and to produce it to a water bailiff if required. Failure to do so carries a maximum penalty of £1000.

The angler does not have to be actually fishing for this requirement to apply. Section 35 of the Act empowers a water bailiff to:

"require a person who is fishing, or whom he reasonably suspects of being about to fish or to have fished within the preceding half hour, to produce his licence and to state his name and address."

If the water bailiff finds that the person does not have a licence he can require him to stop fishing until he has purchased one.

19.5 Angler's proof of identity

Under section 35 (see above) a water bailiff can demand that an angler produce his licence and give him his name and address. If the water bailiff does not know the person, which is probable, he will ask him to produce some form of documentation to verify his identity. This can include a driving licence, a D.S.S. benefit book, or personal documents bearing the person's name and address. The fishing licence on its own may not be acceptable if the water bailiff suspects that it could have been stolen or that it belonged to someone else.

A cheque book would be unsatisfactory as it only gives the account holder's name but not his address – and subsequent enquires at the branch of the bank where the account is held would probably result in the information required not being divulged.

If two persons are fishing near one another, who are suspected of not having licences, the identification of one by the other, and vice versa, would be unacceptable, unless other evidence was forthcoming, as prior collusion on the giving of wrong names and addresses could have been arranged.

A water bailiff has other powers to help him identify a person which can be quite drastic if used (see "Powers of arrest" below) – to obviate the need for this an angler who cannot prove his identity at the waterside but who is otherwise fishing legally, e.g. he has left his licence at home, can volunteer to accompany the water bailiff to a police station where the necessary identification can be established.

19.6 Refusal to cooperate with a water bailiff

There will always be someone who, when found committing an offence, will try to bluff his way out, be deliberately obstructive or adopt a threatening attitude towards a bailiff. This situation has been recognised for many years and most of the earlier, as well as the present, legislation provides the necessary backing to enable it to be dealt with.

The 1975 Act makes it an offence for anyone to refuse to allow a water bailiff to exercise his powers. Section 31(2) of the Act states:-

> "If any person refuses to allow a water bailiff to make any entry, search or examination, which he is authorised to make, or resists or obstructs a water bailiff in any such entry, search, examination or seizure he shall be guilty of an offence".

From this it will be apparent that if a person refuses to cooperate with a water bailiff who is carrying out his duties and exercising his powers that person commits an offence, the penalty for which, on conviction, is a maximum fine of £1000.

19.7 Seizure of tackle and fish

Section 31 of the Act gives a water bailiff the power of seizure of anything being used, or fish taken, in contravention of the Act.

Where the need arises the rod, reel and line, terminal tackle, illegal bait and any fish in the suspect's possession could be seized. (It should be noted that the rod and line of an angler who does not have a valid fishing licence can be seized, as an unlicensed instrument is an illegal instrument within the meaning of the Act).

If the angler had hidden a fish caught illegally in some form of container, such as a bag or sack, that would also be liable to seizure.

If any outer clothing which the angler was wearing was seen to have fish scales on it, or was in any other way relevant to the incident, that too could be seized as evidence and, if necessary, subjected to forensic examination.

The water bailiff will issue a receipt for anything that is seized on which a detailed description of each item will be entered. If no receipt is offered demand one.

As stated earlier never hand anything over to a person claiming to be a water bailiff unless he can produce his warrant.

19.8 Custody and disposal of seized items

The responsibility for anything seized by a water bailiff rests with him and it must be kept in safe custody until such times as its disposal is determined by a court or otherwise.

If it is decided that no proceedings will be taken, anything seized will be returned.

Should it be decided to prosecute, the seized items will be retained to be produced as evidence if required. Items seized and not required as evidence will be returned to their owner as soon as possible.

The court, if it finds the case against the offender proved, can make an order for the forfeiture of any item seized which means that it will not be returned to its owner – but this is usually only in respect of the actual instrument used in the offence and any fish taken. Other seized items would be returned.

If any item is later returned to its owner in a damaged condition a claim can be made against the person responsible for its custody:

it is for this reason that an item seized will be closely examined at the time of seizure and details of any damage entered upon the receipt. This provides evidence of its condition at the time should any claim be made at a later date.

Fish which are seized can be preserved to be presented as evidence in court, or sold, provided they are not unclean, immature or out of season (in which case they will in all probability have been photographed before disposal to provide a visual record for the court). The sale of fish is usually confined to cases involving salmon or sea-trout, which have a high market value.

The proceeds of the sale will be retained until the case is heard when, if the defendant is found Not Guilty, he will have them returned to him. Any fish seized would also be returned after a Not Guilty verdict.

Should the court find him Guilty it could make either the fish or the money subject of a forfeiture order.

19.9 Seizure of a vehicle or boat

A water bailiff can seize a vehicle or boat used in the commission of, or in connection with, a fishery offence and this can be forfeited under an order of the court – but this does not apply to an offence involving the unlicensed use of a rod and line. However, an angler, whether he had a licence or not, who tried to take fish by unconventional means when using a rod e.g. by foul-hooking, could have his car seized if caught as the way in which the rod was being used would classify it as a prohibited instrument and not as an unlicensed one. The power to order the forfeiture of a vehicle or boat was previously confined to the Crown Court but under the Criminal Justice Act 1988 this power has now been extended to a magistrates' court.

19.10 Search of premises

A water bailiff's powers of entry do not extend to a dwelling house, or the curtilage of a dwelling house, unless invited, but if he has reasonable grounds for suspecting that fish which have been taken illegally, or illegal nets or other instruments, are on the property he can apply to a Justice of the Peace, under section 33 of the Act, for a warrant to search the premises. The warrant, if granted, remains operative for seven days and gives him the power to enter and search.

A water bailiff is not given the automatic power to enter onto
land used exclusively for the preservation of wild fowl, or Crown
property. However, should the need arise for him to do so he
can apply to a Justice of the Peace for an Order. This, if granted,
authorises him to enter and remain on the land for up to 24
hours.

19.11 Powers of arrest

Under section 34 of the Act a water bailiff can arrest anyone
fishing illegally between:

> "the end of the first hour after sunset and the beginning of
> the last hour before sunrise"

– this would include a person angling who did not have a licence.

It will be noted that this power only applies at night but this
does not mean that a water bailiff is powerless to arrest at other
times. Section 36 deems him to be a constable which then enables
him to use the general arrest provisions of the Police and Criminal
Evidence Act 1984.

This means that a water bailiff can arrest a person whom he
reasonably suspects of committing, or of having committed, an
offence under the 1975 Act, if:-

> "(a) the name and address of the person is not known and
> cannot be readily ascertained;
> or
> (b) the person fails to give a satisfactory address at which a
> summons can be served;
> or
> (c) the water bailiff has reasonable grounds for doubting that:
>   (i) the name furnished is his real name, or
>   (ii) the address furnished is a satisfactory address at which
>   a summons can be served."

Reasonable force can be used to make an arrest and the arrested
person can be searched.

The arrested person must be taken to a police station. The
purpose of this is to help establish the identity of the suspect,
but should an arrested person be able to satisfy a water bailiff
as to his identity before they reach a police station he can be
released.

A water bailiff also has powers of arrest under the common law.

19.12 Assault on a water bailiff

From time to time water bailiffs are assaulted when carrying out their duties.

It is not suggested that anglers are the main culprits – but should one "lose his marbles" and strike, or attempt to strike, a water bailiff he would have, in fact, "assaulted a constable in the execution of his duty" which is an offence under section 51 of the Police Act 1964. The power of arrest for an offence under this Act comes from the common law.

The offence, if dealt with in a magistrates' court, carries a maximum penalty of a six months prison sentence, or a fine, or both. Should it be a serious assault it could be sent to the Crown Court for trial or sentence, where the maximum penalty rises to two years in prison, or a fine, or both.

19.13 Action if caught breaking the law

Probably the most unwise thing a person who has been caught breaking the law can do, is to "fly off the handle" as this can lead to him doing and saying things which may well make the position much worse.

Most offenders know they have done wrong once the offence has been pointed out to them and to argue at this point is usually futile.

The best advice that can be given to a person in this position is to stay cool, cooperate with the bailiff as fully as the law requires him to do, give him any details that he asks for and hand over any items liable to be seized. (Remember that giving a wrong name and/or address or refusing to hand over anything liable to seizure are additional offences, and that the first can lead to arrest).

The water bailiff is obliged to caution a suspect and give him the chance to explain his actions – in this context the suspect can ask to make a written statement in which the facts, as he sees them, can be recorded together with any excuse or explanation he considers important that could establish his innocence and prevent further action being taken. The statement, which he can write himself or dictate, can be quite brief, in which case it will probably be entered in the water bailiff's note book, or it can be a formal document – in either case check what has been written and only sign it if it is correct.

Finally, ask the water bailiff for his name and the address of his office.

Chapter 20

THE PROCESSES OF LAW

20.1 Consideration of offence

The fact that an angler has broken the law and been caught by a water bailiff does not mean that he will be automatically prosecuted for the offence.

The water bailiff dealing with the offence submits a report on the incident, in which he lists the offences alleged to have been committed, to his superior who checks the validity of the content for any legal or procedural weaknesses. The records are then searched to find if the person concerned has any previous convictions for fishery offences. Depending upon the outcome of the search, the content of the report, the severity of the offence, and the policy which applies, he makes a recommendation as to the course of action that should be followed which he passes to a solicitor. The recommendation may take one of the following forms:-

(a) that no action be taken;
(b) that a letter be sent to the person warning him that no action will be taken in this case but that any future alleged offence will be dealt with more severely; or
(c) that the person be prosecuted.

The solicitor then considers the report and the recommendation. If he agrees that a prosecution should follow he will then decide which of the alleged offences, if there are more than one, should be proceeded with – he may also decide, from reading the report, that another offence was committed at the time which was not apparent to the water bailiff and that this, too, should be included.

The solicitor can then decide in which way the case will be dealt with. Simple cases, e.g. involving licence offences, where the probable plea will be "Guilty", can be dealt with under the Magistrates' Courts Act procedure, whereas more serious offences would be dealt with by a court summons.

20.2 The Magistrates Court Act procedure (M.C.A.)

This does not require the defendant to appear in court if he wishes to plead "Guilty" but allows him to do so by letter to the court.
He is sent the following documents:-

1. a statement in which the procedure is explained and the options open to him are listed. These are that he can:
   (a) plead "Guilty" on a special form (see 4 below) and not appear in court,
   (b) appear in court and plead "Guilty",
   (c) appear in court and plead "Not Guilty".

If he does not reply to the summons, the court can hear the case in his absence;

2. a statement of facts which is the evidence against him and is the only evidence that the court would allow in his absence;
3. a form on which to plead "Guilty"; he can also use this to give any mitigating circumstances which could influence the penalty of the court;
4. a form on which the receipt for the summons is acknowledged; and
5. a list of any of his previous convictions to which it is intended to draw the attention of the court. These can only be quoted in court if he has been sent a copy of the list or if he appears in court in person.

20.3 Court summons

The summons is a document served on the defendant by a court. It gives details of the charge or charges made against him and requires him to present himself before the court, on a date and at the time shown in the summons, in order to answer them. Failure to obey a summons would be a contempt of court for which an additional penalty could be imposed.

A summons can be served personally on the defendant, usually by a water bailiff or police officer, or more often by being sent to him by recorded delivery post.

20.4 Responding to a summons

Whether a summons is served personally, by post or under the M.C.A. procedure it should always be thoroughly checked to:-

(a) make certain that the name on it is correct – poachers have been known to give the name and address of innocent persons;
(b) see if the date of the alleged offence is correct;
(c) see what offences one is being charged with; and
(d) find out the time and place of the hearing.

(If a defendant wanted to plead "Not Guilty" and the date of the hearing was inconvenient the court could, within reason, adjourn it until later provided it was given adequate notice).

In the majority of cases an individual who has been caught committing an offence will find the serving of a summons not unexpected and, provided he realises his position and is aware that he has committed the offence, will probably save himself a lot of time and money by pleading "Guilty".

If the summons is served under the M.C.A. procedure he can do this on the form provided – otherwise he can write to the Clerk of the Court pleading "Guilty", including an apology and giving details of any extenuating circumstances.

Should the defendant wish, he can attend the court and plead "Guilty" in person.

There will be occasions when a defendant would wish to dispute the charges and plead "Not Guilty"; if so, except in the simplest case, he would be advised to seek legal advice by consulting a solicitor.

20.5 Court procedure

Initially, all fishery offence cases are dealt with "summarily", i.e. by a magistrates' court. Most will proceed no further but a few will go on to be heard on "indictment", i.e. by the Crown Court. In both courts, however, the basic procedures, which have been established for many years, are the same – both the defendant and the prosecution are given equal opportunities to present their case, call witnesses and question the evidence of the other side.

In the Crown Court the evidence is heard by a judge and jury. Whilst the former guides the proceedings and passes sentence, it is the latter who decide the verdict based upon the evidence that they have heard.

In a magistrates' court the evidence is heard by lay (non-professional) magistrates, collectively referred to as the Bench, who deliberate on it and arrive at a verdict. The work of the court and the conduct of proceeding, to ensure that no injustices occur, is the responsibility of its clerk who is a qualified lawyer and can advise the Bench on points of law. In this capacity he can also help anyone, not represented by a solicitor, to present his case in the approved manner.

For the rest of this chapter, unless stated otherwise, the proceedings referred to take place summarily.

At the start of the case, the defendant's name is called when, if he is present, he presents himself before the Bench when the charges are read out by the clerk of the court.

If the charges are of a serious nature, the clerk will explain that the defendant has the right to elect for summary trial by the magistrates, or be tried in the Crown Court by a judge and jury. He will also be told that if he elects for summary trial, i.e. by the magistrates, and is found "Guilty" the Bench might consider that the maximum penalty it can award is insufficient to meet the seriousness of the offence. If this is the case, the defendant can be sent to the Crown Court for sentence. In some very serious cases the prosecution will ask that the case be referred to the Crown Court.

Assuming that the defendant elects to be tried summarily he will be asked whether he pleads "Guilty" or "Not Guilty" to each of the charges (if there are more than one) in turn.

If the defendant pleads "Guilty" and is present in court, the usual procedure is for the prosecuting solicitor to read out the statement of facts and a list of any previous convictions – which the defendant can challenge if he wishes. If he pleads "Guilty" by post these can only be cited if he has been notified in writing beforehand of the intention to do so. Having heard the evidence the Bench decides upon an appropriate penalty.

When a "Not Guilty" plea is entered the proceedings open by the prosecution representative outlining the case and calling its witnesses to give their evidence on Oath. When each witness has finished giving evidence the defendant or his solicitor can cross-examine him on it.

When all the prosecution witnesses have been called the defendant has the option of saying nothing, making a statement without taking the Oath or giving his evidence under Oath – on which he can be cross examined.

He can also call any witnesses to give evidence on Oath which would help corroborate his evidence or support his case.

If the defendant or any witnesses he calls give evidence under Oath, they can be cross-examined by the prosecution.

When the defendant and any of his witnesses have finished giving their evidence the Bench retires to consider the facts and to reach a verdict.

The verdict can be "Guilty" or "Not Guilty". If it is the latter, the defendant is free to leave the court with an unblemished character.

If the verdict is "Guilty" verdict, before any penalty is imposed, the Bench will enquire about any previous convictions and, if there are any, these will be read out.

The Bench will also ask the defendant if he has anything to say by way of mitigation – which gives him the opportunity to express his apologies and regrets for the offence – and it may question him about his financial status.

When it has all the relevant information the Bench confers to to decide on a suitable penalty and whether to make an order for the confiscation of any fish or instrument involved in the case.

If a fine is imposed the defendant may request time in which to pay it off.

20.6 Penalties

The maximum penalties that apply in 1989, which courts can impose for fishery offences under the various Acts, are summarised in Figure 3. These are amended from time to time – usually upwards! Note that magistrates and Crown Courts both have the power to impose a prison sentence, a fine or both but the maximum penalties of the latter are much more severe.

Under the Criminal Justice Act 1988, either court can now make an order for the confiscation of any vehicle or vessel used in the commission of, or in connection with, the offence.

Not all the penalties that a court can impose involve imprisonment or a fine – it can give an offender a "conditional discharge" which remains in force for a stipulated period. This means that the court does not impose any penalty but if the defendant appears later in any court for some other offence, while still under a conditional discharge, the circumstances under which the conditional discharge was made can be taken into account when passing sentence.

Sometimes the nature of the offence is such that, although the defendant has pleaded, or been found, "Guilty" the court feels no penalty is called for. In such cases it can award an "absolute discharge", which is a conviction.

If the court is of the opinion that none of the foregoing penalties are appropriate, it may sentence an offender to a period of community service, under which he must carry out work for the benefit of the community under the supervision of an approved person.

Under the Water Act 1989, for offences committed under the 1975 and 1986 Acts, a court may order that any fishing or general licence held by the offender shall be forfeited, and that he shall be disqualified from holding and obtaining a fishing or general licence for a period not exceeding five years as the court thinks fit.

Even if it imposes no monetary penalty e.g by awarding a conditional or absolute discharge, a court can order an offender who is found "Guilty", to contribute towards the cost of bringing the case. If a person is found "Not Guilty" under certain circumstances he may be awarded costs against the prosecution.

20.7 Appeal against conviction or penalty

If a person feels that he has been wrongly convicted, or that his sentence is too great, he can, under certain circumstances, appeal to a superior court e.g where the conviction was in a magistrates' court the appeal would be to the Crown Court.

If considering whether to appeal or not the matter, its implications and likely outcome must be discussed in consultation with a solicitor.

An appeal can be costly, as it also involves the services of a barrister, and, in addition, the court hearing the appeal can, if it sees fit actually increase the original penalty.

MAXIMUM PENALTIES FOR FISHERY OFFENCES

SECTION OF 1975 ACT	OFFENCE	MODE OF PROSECUTION	MAXIMUM PENALTY
1	USING PROHIBITED INSTRUMENTS	SUMMARILY INDICTMENT	. . 3 MONTHS, £2000 OR BOTH. . . 2 YEARS, A FINE OR BOTH.
4	DISCHARGE OF POISONOUS MATTER	SUMMARILY INDICTMENT	. . £2000 + £40 FOR EACH DAY ON WHICH THE OFFENCE CONTINUES AFTER CONVICTION . . 2 YEARS, A FINE OR BOTH.
5(1)	USE OF POISONS, EXPLOSIVES OR ELECTRICAL DEVICES	SUMMARILY INDICTMENT	. . . . £2000. . . 2 YEARS, A FINE OR BOTH.
5(3)	DESTROYING OR DAMAGING DAMS ETC.	SUMMARILY INDICTMENT	. . . . £2000. . . 2 YEARS, A FINE OR BOTH.
19	FISHING IN THE CLOSE SEASON ETC.	SUMMARILY	. . . . £1000.
27	FISHING WITHOUT A LICENCE (ROD AND LINE)	SUMMARILY	. . . . £1000.
	FISHING WITHOUT A LICENCE (OTHER METHODS)	SUMMARILY INDICTMENT	. . 3 MONTHS, £2000 OR BOTH. . . 2 YEARS, A FINE OR BOTH.
	OTHER OFFENCES AND BYELAWS UNDER THE 1975 ACT.	SUMMARILY	. . . . £1000.

SALMON ACT 1986

Sect.32.	HANDLING SALMON IN SUSPICIOUS CIRCUMSTANCES	SUMMARILY INDICTMENT	. . 3 MONTHS, £2000 OR BOTH. . . 2 YEARS, A FINE OR BOTH.

CRIMINAL JUSTICE ACT 1988

MAGISTRATES' COURTS ARE NOW GIVEN ADDITIONAL POWERS TO ORDER THE CONFISCATION OF A VEHICLE OR VESSEL USED IN CONNECTION WITH, OR IN THE COMMISSION OF, A FISHERY OFFENCE.

WATER ACT 1989

WITHDRAWAL OF LICENCE AND DISQUALIFICATION FROM HOLDING A FISHING LICENCE FOR UP TO FIVE YEARS.

Figure 3

Part 2

SCOTLAND

Chapter 21

INTRODUCTION

21.1 Scottish fishery law

As explained earlier (See pages 8-9) Scottish law has its own independent roots.

Scottish common law and the law of property, which covers fishery ownership, varies greatly from that south of the border – yet the content and intentions of Scottish statute law, which is contained in the various fishery Acts, has much in common with that of England and Wales, although in terms of wording and interpretation there are differences.

In England and Wales the proliferation of earlier fishery law, whose history goes back almost to Magna Carta, has largely been consolidated (but not necessarily brought up to date!) by the Salmon and Freshwater Fisheries Act 1975 (as amended by the Salmon Act 1986), which, despite its shortcomings, has the redeeming feature of providing one main source of reference.

In Scotland no such consolidation has occurred, consequently there are in existence a great many Acts – some of which go back well over a hundred years – whose provisions, either in part or in total, still apply and have to be observed.

Both the Scottish and English laws contain many anachronisms and weaknesses of content and draft that, despite subsequent amendments, still leave much to be desired. Perhaps the time will come, in the not too distant future, when the best features of both can be consolidated and integrated to provide one comprehensive modern Act that will be easily understood and universally applied.

This part of the book deals with some of the aspects of Scottish fisheries law and draws attention to its main provisions and the differences between it and that of England and Wales.

21.2 Definitions

In the context of fishery ownership and fishery law generally the following terms and their definitions, which originate in the Scottish legislation, apply:

*"Salmon" means salmon and sea trout as well as the younger stages of both species.

*"Trout" means non-migratory brown trout; it does not include rainbow trout or any other introduced "trout" species.

*"Freshwater fish" means all fish living in freshwater including trout and eels but not salmon, sea trout or fish which migrate between the sea and river such as flounders and shad.

"Fish" is not defined in the legislation and the meaning may be qualified by the context – but when unqualified usually means all species of fish.

"Proprietor" means "any person, partnership, company or corporation which is the proprietor of a salmon fishery or which receives or is entitled to receive the rents of such fishery on its own account or as trustee, guardian or factor for any person, company or corporation" (section 40, Salmon Act 1986).

"Riparian owner" means the owner of the land adjoining a river or loch.

* The definitions of the various kinds of fish differ from those used in legislation in England and Wales where the term "salmon" does not include sea trout but the term "trout" does (except in the context of the Salmon Act 1986!) – and the term "freshwater fish" does not include trout (See section 41 of the 1975 Act).

Chapter 22

FISHERY OWNERSHIP

22.1 History of ownership of salmon fisheries

Prior to it becoming part of the United Kingdom, under the Act of Union in 1707, Scotland existed as an independent feudal kingdom with its own laws and legal system that had evolved to meet the circumstances which existed there: these differed in many respects from those of England and Wales which were united earlier by the Act of Union of 1536. After 1707 much of the Scottish law and legal system was retained and this is reflected in the law as it effects the ownership of fisheries.

The law of fishery ownership originates in the common law where it is regarded as property but the major difference between the two legal systems is that, in England and Wales, under Magna Carta the right of the public to fish in tidal waters was established. However, in Scotland under a ruling of the courts in the case of the *Commissioners of Woods and Forests* v. *Gammell* in 1859 it was held that the salmon fishing rights in freshwater and the sea around Scotland was a separate heritable tenement vested in the Crown unless expressly or constructively granted to a subject.

Therefore there is no public right of fishery for salmon anywhere in Scotland including coastal waters.

Most of the Crown fisheries, including those in coastal waters, are administered by the Crown Estate Commissioners, and are let to individuals or bodies.

Where an independent private fishery exists at the present time the owner gets his title to it directly or indirectly from a grant made by the Crown. Such fisheries are described in legal terms as a "separate feudal estate" that can exist independently of land.

The position in Orkney and Shetland is different.

In his book *Fishing in Scotland*, (W. Green and Son), The Hon. Lord Jauncey writes:-

"The right of salmon-fishing in those islands depends not upon feudal law as in the rest of Scotland but upon udal law which is a survival of the ancient Norse law. The right of salmon fishing belongs to the owners of the lands adjoining the waters concerned, unless it has been transferred by contract, and it is not a right vested in the Crown."

In tidal waters the position is less clear and subject to dispute – the matter has yet to be satisfactorily resolved.

22.2 Freshwater fisheries

As a general rule the freshwater fisheries of Scotland are not held in such high esteem as are its salmon fisheries.

Freshwater fisheries in non-tidal waters are deemed *not* to be a "separate feudal estate" and, therefore, to belong to the riparian owner. These fisheries cannot be owned by a person who does not own the land – unlike the position in England and Wales – but they can be leased and the lease can be binding on any future owner of the riparian rights. The lessee does not need to have any association with the adjoining land. There are some exceptions to this, e.g. on Loch Leven and the Lake of Monteith, where the rights have been separated by private Act of Parliament.

On a loch where there is more than one riparian owner each has the exclusive right to fish from his own property but can also fish any part of the loch from a boat.

The fish which occur naturally in a loch or river belong to no one until they are caught, when they become the property of the captor: on an artificially stocked water it is possible that they belong to the owner and that anyone who takes them without permission could be guilty of theft. Compare this with the position in England and Wales under the Theft Act 1968.

22.3 Public fisheries

There is a public right of fishery for sea-fish and freshwater fish in navigable tidal waters, which includes river estuaries and lochs that are subject to the influence of the tides – although the position in Orkney and Shetland is less clear. Anyone who is in doubt should seek local advice particularly on lochs which extend many miles inland and give the impression of being non-tidal.

22.4 River boundaries

The boundary between fisheries on opposite banks of a river is the centre line of that river, unless any deed or agreement shows otherwise, (a situation similar to that in England and Wales) but this does not mean that an angler can only fish his half of the river. In the case of *Fotheringham* v. *Kerr or Passmore* the House of Lords ruled in 1984 that

"Where the opposite banks of a Scottish river were in different ownerships, each proprietor was entitled to stand on his own bank, or to wade out to the limit of his property in the bed of the river (the 'medium filum' or middle line) and to fish as far across the river as he could reach by normal casting or spinning. He was not restricted to casting or spinning only up to the medium filum."

This suggests that an angler can fish the whole width of a river provided that he does so from his own half.

However, the position has been further complicated. In the High Court in March 1990 involving a dispute over a fishery on the Tweed, the Judge ruled that in the case where the centre of the river was not only the boundary between fisheries but also the boundary between England and Scotland, anglers fishing on the Scottish side were restricted to their own half of the river and that even if they were to cast into the other half from their own side they would still commit a trespass.

It should be noted that this judgment refers to Scottish rivers only and that its application to rivers in England and Wales has yet to be accepted (see also 4.6).

22.5 Proprietor's rights

The right to fish does not give a proprietor ownership of the fish in the river, as these are deemed to be wild creatures and to belong to no one until they are caught when they become the property of the captor.

Where a fishery exists independently of the adjoining land the proprietor may claim certain rights to allow him to use the fishery. These may include access for himself and any vehicle that is needed to carry his fishing gear – which may involve traversing land belonging to a riparian owner to get to the water – and to fish from either bank. The access is for a specific purpose only and is usually by an agreed route or routes – although in a recent case, which applied to a specific fishery only, the so called "right of access" was ajudged to be on the sufferance of the riparian owner. Conversely, the riparian owners cannot erect anything which would interfere with the operation of the fishery.

Where proprietors are also riparian owners of opposite banks of a river that separates their property, both have fishing rights, but they can only exercise those rights from their own side of the river.

The owner of a salmon fishery has the right to dispose of it or manage it as he sees fit – subject to any statutory provisions and common law obligations to his neighbours. He can sell it, lease it on a long term basis, permit individuals to fish it on payment of a fee or fish it himself.

The right to fish for salmon also includes the right to fish for freshwater fish – but this is not an exclusive right as it is shared with the riparian owner if he is not the proprietor of the salmon fishery.

22.6 Dual fishery ownership

As a salmon fishery can exist independently of any land adjoining (although in many cases the fishery is associated with it) it can be fished by the proprietor without reference to the riparian owner. But the riparian owner owns a freshwater fishing right in the water and can exercise it without reference to the salmon fishery proprietor – thus two fisheries can exist on the same stretch of water. Indeed, since the salmon fishing rights include a subsidiary right to fish for freshwater fish, both parties have independent rights to fish for those species. The general rule is that, in exercising their rights, the fishermen must have regard to the rights of others and not be activated by a spirit of rivalry towards them.

Chapter 23

PERMISSION TO FISH

23.1 Angler's responsibility

While the public at large may have access to a river or non-tidal loch this does not bequeath the right to fish.

Anyone wishing to fish for either salmon (in both tidal and non-tidal waters) or freshwater fish must first obtain permission from the proprietor or riparian owner, as appropriate, before beginning to fish.

There are certain legal requirements, in relation to fishing permission – these differ between salmon and freshwater fish – that an angler must observe and which are explained below.

23.2 The legal position for salmon

Permission to fish for salmon must be in writing. To fish in any inland waters or the sea within one mile of the low-water mark without this permission is an offence under section 1 of the Salmon and Freshwater Fisheries (Protection) (Scotland) Act 1951 which carries a maximum penalty of £400.

This is in marked contrast to the situation in England and Wales where fishing without permission is dealt with under the Theft Act 1968 whose provisions, which cover non-tidal waters only, do not extend to Scotland.

23.3 Sunday fishing

One aspect of salmon fishing, not often realised by a visitor, is that Sunday fishing for salmon and sea-trout by rod and line is prohibited between midnight on Saturday and midnight on Sunday.

Some riparian owners may refuse to give permission to fish for trout or other freshwater fish on Sundays. If intending to fish over a week-end always check with the fishery beforehand to determine the position.

23.4 The legal position for freshwater fish

There is no general statutory offence in Scotland of fishing for
freshwater fish without a permit but anyone who does so may
be turned off the water by the proprietor, riparian owner or agent
of either "without undue violence". This is again in contrast to
the position in England and Wales where to fish for any species
of fish without a permit in a private fishery is an offence.

If he has caused any damage in the course of his escapade
he may find himself liable under the civil law to make reparations.
Again it must be stressed that the public at large does not have
a right to fish for freshwater fish without permission except in
the tidal part of a river or a sea-loch.

An exception to the above arises on rivers and their tributaries
(other than the River Annan) that run into the Solway Firth, where
to fish for salmon *or other fish* without permission is a statutory
offence under section 9 of the Solway Act 1804.

In addition, under section 1 of the Freshwater and Salmon
Fisheries (Scotland) Act 1976, the Secretary of State may make
a Protection Order for part or the whole of a river system and
it is an offence to fish for freshwater fish in such an area without
legal right or written permission – this carries a maximum penalty
of £400.

There are currently five Protection Orders in force – these are:

(a) The Tweed and Eye Protection Order 1980,
(b) The Upper Spey and Associated Waters Protection Order 1982,
(c) The River Tummel Catchment Area Protection Order 1983,
(d) The River Lunan Catchment Area Protection Order 1983, and
(e) The River Tay Catchment Area Protection Order 1986.

Compare the above with the position in England and Wales
where fishing for any species of fish in a private fishery without
permission is an offence under the Theft Act 1968.

23.5 Obtaining permission

Salmon fishing is controlled by the proprietors, who include
farmers, individuals, estates, hotels and angling associations, and
it is to these bodies or individuals that one should turn in order
to get permission to fish.

Some proprietors may be prepared to allow the casual angler
to fish on payment (and there are some excellent fisheries which

do this if one can find them) but these are probably in the minority as in most cases the fishing has been let for a season to an individual or syndicate. Most of the angling associations, however, will assist a visiting angler for a short term and all hotels with fishing make this available to their guests – but it is always advisable to book up in advance rather than to arrive unannounced and expect to be accommodated.

If trout, or other freshwater fish, are the main quarry permission should be sought from the proprietors (even though salmon fishing may not be possible on their fisheries, many will allow fishing for trout) or the riparian owners. There is a commonly held belief that one does not need to have permission to fish for these species – this is a mistake as anyone who fishes must obtain permission before he starts.

23.6 Permit cost

Many riparian owners and proprietors will give permission to fish for trout or other freshwater fish without making a charge or, if one is made, it is usually nominal. However, on lochs where a trout fishery is specially preserved and stocked, a charge in keeping with the quality of the fishery can be expected.

In the case of salmon fishing, particularly on the better beats of major rivers, the cost of fishing for a season could run into many hundreds or even thousands of pounds depending on the quality. If day permits were available on these fisheries the cost would be proportionally high. On lesser rivers, which can and do provide excellent sport at the right time of the year, and on many angling association waters the cost of a day's fishing could be a few pounds.

23.7 The accidental catching of sea trout

The majority of Scottish rivers have a run of sea trout which can, and do, take the bait, fly or lure used by an angler who is after brown trout which inhabit the same waters.

In Scotland the term "salmon" includes sea trout and an angler who did not have permission to fish for salmon would, if he kept the fish, have committed the offence of fishing without written permission under section 1 of the 1951 Act. In such a case the wise thing to do would be to return it to the water. Some owners give written permission to fish for trout on the under-

standing that an angler catching a salmon accidentally gives it
to the owner.

On the Tweed this position has been regularised. An angler
would be expected to deliver to the owner of a salmon fishery
any salmon caught on that fishery while trout fishing – to fail
to do so would be an offence under section 73 of the Tweed
Fisheries Act 1857.

23.8 Fishing for coarse fish

Scotland is usually regarded as having only salmon and trout
fishing. This is a misconception as there are many rivers and
lochs which can provide excellent sport for the angler who seeks
other kinds of fish such as grayling, pike etc. – the so called
coarse fish. Some rivers, such as the Tweed and its tributaries,
offers a wide selection of species that are equal to many rivers
south of the Border.

These come within the meaning of freshwater fish and the
same procedure as for trout fishing should be observed. Permission should be sought from either a proprietor or a riparian owner
before starting to fish.

On some fisheries these species are regarded as pests and the
owners are only too pleased to have them removed – but it should
be noted that the use of set lines, including fixed rods, is strictly
speaking unlawful for any species.

23.9 Sea fishing

Apart from the question of access to tidal waters over private
land or property, there are virtually no restrictions on angling
for sea fish. Many tidal lochs provide excellent sport and this
can be a little disconcerting to the angler who catches saithe (coal-
fish) in what appears to be a fresh-water loch miles away from
the open sea.

23.10 An angler's obligations

If granted permission to fish there are are both legal and customary
requirements that have to be observed.

The legal requirements place upon an angler the duty to comply
with the provisions of the various fishery Acts and regulations
which include the need, if salmon fishing, to have a written permit

which he will be expected to carry and to produce when required to do so.

Although a written permit is not necessary to fish for trout or other freshwater fish (except in an area covered by a Protection Order) it would be expedient to ask the person giving permission to provide one.

Among the customary requirements, he may be restricted in the way he fishes by the proprietor or riparian owner, some of whom allow certain methods only, such as fly fishing, spinning etc.; their wishes must be complied with.

If the fishery is divided into beats the angler will be expected to fish only on the beat that has been allocated to him or, where the beats operate on a rolling basis, to move to the next beat at a prearranged time.

On large salmon rivers where a boat is provided the angler may be expected to make use of the services of a ghillie who acts both as boatman and mentor – and will be expected to suitably reward him at the end of the day. The person who fails to take advantage of this service usually does so to his detriment.

Most proprietors keep accurate records of the catches on their waters and require anglers to weigh-in all fish caught and enter the details in a catch-book.

Although not specifically referred to, an angler will be expected to observe all the usual courtesies towards others fishing the water – however, there may be other things expected or required of him which will be made known at the time when permission is granted.

23.11　Breaking the terms of a permit

The terms under which permission is granted are part of a contract between the angler and the owner or occupier of the fishery. If the terms are ignored or broken it would appear that the permission would be invalidated and under these circumstances, if the angler was fishing for salmon, he might be caught by section 1 of the 1951 Act, i.e. fishing without legal right or written permission.

If he was fishing for any species of fish in an area covered by a Protection Order it could be argued that he might be caught by section 1 of the 1976 Act (See above). If fishing for trout or freshwater fish elsewhere, the breach of the contract would be a civil not criminal matter and the angler could be required to leave the fishery.

Compare this with the position in England and Wales where an offence under the Theft Act 1968 would have been committed in each case.

Chapter 24

FISHERY LAW AND ENFORCEMENT*

24.1 Scottish fishery legislation

The Acts which deal with the salmon, trout and freshwater fisheries of Scotland go back over several hundred years and include the following:-

The Theft Act 1607
The Solway Act 1804
The Tweed Fisheries Act 1857
The Tweed Fisheries Amendment Act 1859
The Salmon Fisheries (Scotland) Act 1868
The Freshwater Fish (Scotland) Act 1902
The Trout (Scotland) Act 1933
The Salmon and Freshwater Fisheries (Protection) (Scotland) Act 1951
The Freshwater and Salmon Fisheries (Scotland) Act 1976
The Salmon Act 1986
(All these Acts will be referred to, henceforth, by the year only).

24.2 Application of the legislation

Not all of the above Acts have a general application throughout Scotland – some only apply locally. Parts of England are dealt with in some of the legislation.

The legislation that applies to the Tweed covers the whole of its catchment, much of which lies south of the border in England where it is exempt from the provisions of the 1975 Act but not from the provisions of the Theft Act 1968 which applies to the whole of England and Wales.

Conversely, the River Esk (and its tributaries) comes under the Salmon and Freshwater Fisheries Act 1975 which applies in

*(This deals with the law only as it affects angling. Other methods are dealt with in the legislation but these are ignored).

131

general to England and Wales but has an application to the Esk
under section 39 of that Act; consequently all future references
to Scottish law in this book will exclude this river.

It is apparent from the foregoing that the law is more diverse
and complicated than in England and Wales and requires a visiting
angler to be particularly careful.

24.3 Administration of Scottish fisheries

The overall responsibility for administering the fisheries rests with
the Secretary of State, working through the Department of Agriculture and Fisheries for Scotland (DAFS).

At a local level there are no multi-purpose bodies, similar to
the regions of the National Rivers Authority in England and Wales,
whose responsibilities include fisheries. Instead, there are one
hundred and eight Salmon Fishery Districts which were established under the Salmon Fisheries (Scotland) Acts 1862-1868. (The
situation is similar to that in England and Wales prior to the
River Board Act 1948 when the fisheries on individual rivers, or
groups of rivers, were managed by conservancy boards whose
sole role was the protection, preservation and conservation of
fisheries).

The fishery districts are maintained by the 1986 Act and can
be altered under it. These vary considerably in area – the Tay
and Kyle of Sutherland districts have catchments of hundreds
of square miles while some of the smaller ones have areas
measured in tens (or less) of square miles.

Within any district the proprietors of the salmon fisheries can
form an association for the purpose of the protection and improvement of the fisheries within their district – this then becomes
the Salmon Fishery Board for that district.

So far, boards have been formed in just over half of the districts
and there are currently 58 in being (See Appendices F and G).

In a district where no board has been formed responsibility
for the fisheries administration rests with the Secretary of State
and enforcement will rest with both the police and persons
authorised by him under the provisions of the 1951 Act.

24.4 Powers of fishery boards

Under the Acts which established them and granted them powers
fishery boards can:-

(a) impose a fishery assessment on each salmon fishery in the district, (this is their main source of income);

(b) do such works and incur such expenses as are expedient for:-

    (i)   protecting and improving the fisheries within the district,

    (ii) the increase of salmon, or

    (iii) the stocking of the waters of the district with salmon;

(c) appoint persons to act as water bailiffs.

The Secretary of State, in consultation with the fishery boards or other interested parties, can make regulations that, inter alia, affect angling within a fishery district. The need for a regulation is usually identified and promoted by the local fishery board.

The fishery boards and the way in which they are managed reflect the views and interests of the proprietors in the district within a framework provided by the legislation. As there are many boards each could have its own regulation – which would be very confusing to a stranger – but in practice the only variable is the annual close time and there could soon be a bait and lures regulation on the Tweed.

24.5 Fishing licences

Licences to fish with a rod and line for any species of fish are not required or issued in Scotland; however, anyone who fishes must have the permission of the fishery owner which, in the case of salmon fishing, must be in writing and must be produced to a water bailiff.

24.6 Fishery board finance

Unlike the situation in England and Wales, where part of the N.R.A.'s fisheries income is derived from licence duties levied on individual anglers and commercial fishermen, a Scottish board gets its money from each of the fisheries in its area by means of a fishery assessment. This is a form of rating whereby a standard rate is set by the board and levied on individual fisheries (which includes commercial fisheries both in rivers and in the sea) in proportion to the value of each.

As most proprietors charge for the right to fish, and the duty to meet their rating responsibilities is often foremost in their minds, the cost is eventually and inevitably passed onto the fishermen!

Chapter 25

FISHING METHODS

25.1 Permitted methods

The only permitted method of fishing in inland waters for salmon and freshwater fish, as defined by section 2 of the 1951 Act, is by net and coble and "single rod and line". As this book only considers angling, fishing by net and coble is ignored.

(Compare this with the position in England and Wales where the only prohibited methods are set out in the 1975 Act).

25.2 Definition of rod and line

The term "rod and line" is defined in the 1951 Act as,

"a single rod and line with such bait or lure as is lawful at the passing of the Act".

Under section 8 of the 1986 Act the Secretary of State can make new or amending regulations, for the purposes of defining "rod and line", specifying or varying baits and lures, and the times and areas where they will apply,

It follows that any bait or lure which is not lawful but which is being used with a rod and line makes the use of the rod and line illegal.

25.3 Prohibited methods

A number of lures and methods of fishing with a rod and line were prohibited by various Acts that were in force when the 1951 Act became operative. These prohibitions were continued in general terms under this Act – but the lures and methods were not specifically listed; thus it is necessary in many cases to refer to the original legislation for clarification (see above).

(In England and Wales the 1975 Act lists the principal methods and instruments which are prohibited and this is reinforced by byelaws).

The provisions of the 1951 Act, in association with the earlier legislation give effect to the following:

(a) A "single rod and line" presupposes that a line used without a rod e.g. a hand line etc. would be illegal.

(b) The use of a set-line - a baited line set and left unattended in a fishery to be recovered later - is illegal. A rod and line not held in the hand (i.e. lying on the bank) has been deemed in law to be a set-line.

(c) Such practices as "sniggering" (foul-hooking or snatching) and the use of "rake hooks" (stroke-hauls) is similarly prohibited. The actual instrument at the end of the line e.g. a devon minnow or mounted prawn, could in other circumstances be legal, but if used to try and impale a fish other than by being taken in the mouth would not be. The usual test employed to determine whether a method is legal is that the bait or lure must be taken by the fish.

(d) The use of an "otter" is prohibited - this could apply to the use of a bubble float with the bait or lure between it and the rod, which could be construed to be an "otter" within the meaning of the Acts.

(e) Provisions are made for a gaff, landing net or tailer to be used as an auxiliary to a rod and line.

(On the Tweed the use of the gaff when fishing for salmon is prohibited in the period between 15 September and 1 May of the following year. Some fishery owners may impose their own restraints on its use at certain times of the year).

To take salmon by any illegal means is an offence under the appropriate Act carrying a maximum penalty of £1000 but there could be a possible alternative offence of "possessing salmon which had been illegally taken, killed or landed" under section 7 of the 1951 Act as amended by section 22 of the 1986 Act. This carries a maximum penalty on summary conviction of "imprisonment for a term not exceeding three months, or to a fine not exceeding the statutory maximum or both". If convicted on indictment the maximum penalty is "imprisonment for a term not exceeding two years, or a fine or both".

Although the subject is dealt with differently under Scottish law the above provisions bear a remarkable likeness to those that apply in England and Wales.

25.4 Illegal baits

The use of any fish roe for the purpose of fishing was prohibited by section 18 of the 1868 Act and although this part of section 18 is now repealed, the use of fish roe is still unlawful by virtue of the terms defining a "rod and line". The maximum penalty for using fish roe is £200.

To be in possession of salmon roe, or to buy or sell it is also an offence for which the maximum penalty is £400.

Local regulations may restrict certain baits or lures to certain times of the year.

25.5 Regulation of the use of baits and methods

Under section 8 of the 1986 Act a fishery board can apply to the Secretary of State to make regulations that specify:

(a) baits and lures or classes of baits and lures that may be used,

(b) times when the regulations apply and,

(c) areas to which the regulations apply.

These regulations are generally of local application only and can affect one district fishery board's area (or part of an area) but not the adjoining one. It follows that the angler who is unfamiliar with an area should take steps to find out what regulations apply before starting to fish; and, of course, individual fishery owners, or groups of owners, may have their own non-statutory rules as to methods allowed on any waters.

Chapter 26

CLOSE TIMES

26.1 The weekly close times for salmon

Salmon fishing starts in the early spring and continues into the autumn but during this period there is a certain time each week when it is not allowed – this is the "weekly close time".

The weekly close time for salmon and sea-trout is established under section 13 of the 1951 Act and applies to the whole of Scotland and all of the Tweed catchment, including that part which lies in England.

It is introduced to help preserve breeding stock by providing a period of respite each week when fish can travel up-river without being subject to fishing pressure; this is achieved by a prohibition on angling for a twenty-four hour period *between midnight on Saturday and midnight on Sunday*.

All other types of fishing for salmon are banned from mid-day on Saturday until six a.m. on the following Monday.

26.2 The annual close time for salmon

The "annual close time" is established to coincide with the main breeding period of the salmon during the autumn and winter and is intended to let the fish spawn without interference. It must be of at least 168 days duration and applies to all methods of fishing – however provision is made within this period to reduce the close season for fishing by means of rod and line.

On the Tweed the annual close time for angling is from 14 September until 15 February of the following year but the use of artificial fly only is allowed from 14 September to 30 November and from 1 February until 15 February.

On the majority of Scottish rivers the annual close time for salmon angling is from 1 November until 10 February following (both dates inclusive) – elsewhere there are local variations of the date on which the annual close time commences, for example on the Aberdeenshire Dee it is 1 October while on the Tweed it is 1 December. It has been said that by moving from area to area an angler could legally fish for salmon in Scotland for most of the year!

(Compare the position in England and Wales where the close seasons are shown in the 1975 Act as the periods between two dates, whereas in Scotland the commencing and finishing dates of the annual close time are given).

26.3 Regulation of close times

The actual duration of the close time for angling and the date on which it begins is specified in byelaws made under the 1862-1868 Acts and may now be amended by order made by the Secretary of State under the provisions of section 6 of the 1986 Act.

A close time order is made at the request of the district fishery board and applies to that district only but it should be noted that different orders in one district can apply to different parts of that district or even to different parts of the same river.

As there are many fishery districts the seasons will vary considerably between various parts of Scotland. A list of current annual angling close times for salmon with rod and line, and the districts where they apply, are shown in Figure 5 – further details can be obtained from:

The Department of Agriculture and Fisheries for Scotland,
Chesser House,
Gorgie Road,
Edinburgh.

26.4 Close times for freshwater fish

The only freshwater fish subject to an annual close time is the brown trout for which angling is prohibited during the period between 6 October and 15 March following – this does not apply to rainbow trout.

Coarse fishing is permitted throughout the year.

26.5 Fishing in the close season

To fish with rod and line for salmon or trout during either the weekly close time (in the case of salmon) and the annual close time in respect of both salmon and trout is an offence under the Acts punishable by a fine and the possible forfeiture of tackle and fish.

In the case of salmon the prohibition relating to the annual close time is under section 15 of the 1868 Act and to the weekly close time (Sunday) under section 13 of the 1951 Act.

ANNUAL CLOSE TIMES FOR ANGLING
FOR SALMON IN SCOTLAND
(Dates shown are inclusive)

Start	End	Districts
Nov 1	Feb 10	All districts except for the following:
Oct 1	Jan 10	Helmsdale, Kyle of Sutherland
Oct 1	Jan 11	Halladale, Strathy, Naver, Borgie, Hope, Polla.
Oct 1	Jan 25	Conon.
Oct 1	Jan 31	Aberdeen Dee.
Oct 1	Feb 10	Nairn, Spey.
Oct 6	Jan 10	Thurso.
Oct 7	Feb 10	Findhorn.
Oct 15	Feb 28	Cree.
Oct 16	Jan 14	Ness, Tay (Except Earn).
Oct 16	Jan 31	Brora.
Oct 16	Feb 10	Awe, Beauly, Lossie, Dunbeath.
Oct 16	Feb 15	Drummachloy (Isle of Bute).
Oct 17	Feb 10	Creed (Isle of Lewis), Loch Roag.
Nov 1	Jan 31	R. Earn, Forth.
Nov 1	Feb 9	Ugie.
Nov 1	Feb 15	Add, Eachaig, North Esk, South Esk, Fyne, Shira, Aray, Ruel.
Nov 1	Feb 24	Bervie, Carradale, Clayburn (Harris), Fincastle, Fleet (Sutherland), Fleet (Kirkcudbright), Girvan, Howmore (South Uist), Inner (Jura), Iorsa (Arran), Irvine and Garnock, Laggan (Islay), Luce, Mullanageren, Orkney Islands, Shetland Islands, Stinchar.
Nov 16	Feb 24	Annan.
Nov 30	Feb 24	Urr.
Dec 1	Jan 31	Tweed.
Dec 1	Feb 24	Nith.

Figure 5

It is an offence to fish for, take or have in possession trout during the annual close time under section 1 of the 1902 Act.

The maximum penalty for fishing for salmon during the weekly close time is £1000 and for fishing for them in the annual close time the maximum penalty is £400. If a salmon was taken and kept a possible alternative offence of "possessing unlawfully taken fish knowing or having reason to suspect that it was illegally taken, killed or landed" under section 22 of the 1986 Act could have been committed. This carries a maximum penalty on summary conviction of "imprisonment for a term not exceeding three months, or to a fine not exceeding the statutory maximum or both." If convicted on indictment the maximum penalty is "imprisonment for a term not exceeding two years, or to a fine or both".

26.6 Sale of salmon and trout

It is an offence under section 21 of the 1868 Act to buy sell or have in one's possession any salmon taken during the annual close time. This, however, does not extend to salmon caught by rod and line during the period when its use is permitted but it is up to the angler to prove that the fish was legally taken by this method.

It is an offence under section 2 of the 1933 Act to sell trout during the period 1 September to 31 March following – both dates inclusive.

Chapter 27

UNCLEAN AND IMMATURE FISH

27.1 Unclean and immature fish

Under both the general legislation and under the Acts which apply to the Tweed, fish which are "unclean" (or "foul" in the case of the Tweed) or "unseasonable" must not be taken. This applies independently of the close times.

A prohibition on the taking of unclean and immature fish is found in both the English and Scottish law but there are differences relating to definition and application between the two codes.

27.2 Definition of an "unclean" salmon

A salmon that has recently spawned and has not recovered from spawning is defined as an "unclean" fish – the general term applied to such a fish is "kelt".

Salmon are considered to be kelts until they have returned to the sea after spawning.

Compare this definition to that in England and Wales where under the 1975 Act the term "unclean" embraces both "unclean" and "unseasonable" (See below).

27.3 Definition of "unseasonable" salmon

An "unseasonable" salmon is one which is gravid and on the point of spawning. It should be noted that a fish can be gravid without being about to spawn (See page 75) – a condition often encountered late in the fishing season.

A simple test is to gently press the fish's belly towards the vent and if eggs or milt are discharged the fish is about to spawn – but be warned, more objective criteria may be applied in some areas.

27.4 Protection of unclean and unseasonable salmon

An unclean or unseasonable salmon can be caught during the fishing season but provided it is returned alive to the water no offence will have been committed. If the fish is not returned an offence of "taking or possessing unclean or unseasonable salmon" is committed under section 20 of the 1868 Act or, in the case of the Tweed, under section 70 of the 1857 Act, carrying a maximum penalty of £400; a further offence comes under section 72 of 1875 Act – that of "neglecting to return foul or unseasonable fish to the river".

A possible alternative offence to any of the above would be one of "possessing unlawfully taken fish knowing or having reason to suspect that it was illegally taken, killed or landed" under section 22 of the 1986 Act . This carries a maximum penalty on summary conviction of "imprisonment for a term not exceeding three months, or to a fine not exceeding the statutory maximum or both". If convicted on indictment the maximum penalty is "imprisonment for a term not exceeding two years, or a fine or both".

27.5 Immature salmon

Immature salmon are the young of the species that have yet to migrate to the sea where they grow to maturity. The term includes "fry", "parr" (which can be confused with brown trout), and "smolts" which can be distinguished by their silvery appearance.

In England and Wales under the 1975 Act an immature salmon is one which is less than 12 inches in length but no such definition appears in the Scottish law. The size below which sea trout (classed as salmon in Scotland) are considered to be immature is not laid down in the 1975 act but is left to the discretion of the Authority.

It is an offence under section 19 of the 1868 Act and section 74 of the 1857 Act to take or kill or be in possession of immature salmon (smolts, parr and fry). The maximum penalty for this offence is £400.

A small male salmon parr – only a few inches in length – can become sexually mature and be involved in the spawning activities of a female many times larger than itself. Of course it is an offence to take parr at any time but if one of these was caught in this condition and not returned an additional offence of "taking or possessing unclean or unseasonable salmon" would have been committed.

27.6 Unclean or immature brown trout

The legislation referring to unclean and unseasonable fish relates to salmon (including migratory trout) only.

There is no statutory minimum size limit below which trout cannot be taken but it is an offence to sell trout which are under 8 inches in length (section 2, 1933 Act).

Where trout are stocked into a loch or river the owner may well impose his own minimum size limits.

27.7 Accidental catching of fish

It is virtually impossible, short of not fishing, to avoid catching, at some time or another, a fish which is immature or unclean within the meaning of the Acts or whose retention would be illegal for any reason. The law recognises this and, should the event occur, takes no action if the fish, be it trout or salmon, is returned immediately to the water with as little injury as possible.

27.8 Removal of dead fish

Only the owner of a fishery or his agent or a person authorised by him may take dead fish from the water. A tenant angler might come under this provision.

A bona-fide angler fishing with the full permission and confidence of a proprietor is unlikely to get into difficulty.

Chapter 28

WATER BAILIFFS

28.1 Fishery law enforcement

Due to the complexity of Scottish law there is no one body responsible for its enforcement, as in England and Wales where this task falls, via the N.R.A. and its regions, to its water bailiffs.

Under the various Scottish Acts and regulations the responsibility for enforcing the law at the water side is divided between:-

(a) The police,
(b) Water bailiffs appointed by the District Fishery Boards under the provisions of section 16 of the 1986 Act,
(c) Secretary of State's Water Bailiffs i.e. persons appointed and authorised by the Secretary of State to act as water bailiffs, under the 1951 Act, and
(d) Wardens appointed by the Secretary of State under the 1976 Act.

The roles and powers of each differ in certain respects to meet the duties which they are required to perform.

28.2 The police

The police, either acting on their own or in association with water bailiffs, play an important and effective role in the enforcement of Scottish fishery law particularly in districts where no fishery board has been established, and where probably they represent the prime deterrent against poachers. They use powers granted by the fishery Acts and the general law.

28.3 Fishery board water bailiffs

A water bailiff appointed by a District Fishery Board under the 1986 Act has the prime role of enforcing the provisions of the fishery legislation in the district of the Board which appointed him. He can also use his powers in adjoining Fishery Districts.

To help him fulfil this role and to enable him to carry out his duties effectively he is given certain powers under the Acts.

In many ways his powers are similar to those of water bailiffs employed by the N.R.A. in England and Wales although he is more restricted in some respects than are his colleagues south of the Border.

As the statutory duties of a fishery board relate primarily to salmon, the powers of a water bailiff in its employment apply basically to that species, but he does have some additional powers in respect of trout fishing, although protecting trout fisheries is not one of his duties. His powers in respect of other species of freshwater fish are extremely limited.

In general terms he has the power of entry, search, seizure and arrest which can be exercised within the area of the Board and in adjoining Board areas. These powers extend to the sea out to three miles from mean low water spring tide mark.

His powers as they affect angling include:

(a) the right to enter at any time and remain on land near a river or the sea for preventing breaches of the various Acts or detecting persons who have committed offences under those Acts;

(b) the examination of any instrument used in fishing or any basket, pocket or other thing which there is reasonable cause to suspect of containing salmon or trout taken illegally;

(c) the seizure of any fish, instrument or article liable to be forfeited under the Acts, (his responsibilities for any items seized are similar to those of water bailiffs south of the border);

(d) the inspection and detention of packages suspected of containing illegally caught salmon or trout; and

(e) the arrest of any person found committing an offence under certain sections of the Act.

As in the 1975 Act in England and Wales, his powers and ability to apply them are reinforced by provisions in the legislation which makes it an offence for anyone to obstruct him in the exercise of those powers.

In addition to his policing role, he may be required to carry out work associated with the improvement of the fisheries such as predator control, and river stocking.

28.4 Secretary of State's water bailiff

In districts in which District Fishery Boards have not been formed there could be a vacuum in the policing of the fisheries unless provision was made for this eventuality.

This is met in part by the Secretary of State appointing persons to exercise the powers of water bailiffs in such areas. Although appointed by the Secretary of State most are nominated for appointment by the proprietors of fisheries, angling associations or other bodies. The role is not full time, as in their ordinary work they are responsible to others. Persons appointed could include ghillies, estate workers etc.

The Secretary of State can also appoint persons to exercise the powers of a water bailiff, who have a fishery policing role over the whole country such as an Inspector of the Fishmongers Company.

In some respects the powers of a person so appointed are more extensive, and in others less so, than those of his fishery board counterpart (for example his area of operation is limited to that in which he is authorised to operate whereas the Board bailiff operates in the District of the Board that appoints him and in immediate adjacent areas) – but as far as the angler is concerned the powers of both are similar.

28.5 Water bailiff's identity document

Both a fishery board and Secretary of State's water bailiff are provided with a letter of appointment or badge of office and which has only to be produced in order to exercise their powers.

Most Scottish water bailiffs do not have an easily recognisable uniform so that initially an angler will have no indication that a person is a water bailiff until that person has identified himself. Even then it is advisable to ask him to substantiate his claim and to produce his letter of appointment or badge of office.

28.6 Warden appointed by the Secretary of State

The 1976 Act provides that, in certain circumstances, the Secretary of State, on the request of fishery owners, may make a protection Order, in respect of a river or part of the catchment of a river, to control fishing activities in the interest of conservation. The owners must show that, if an Order is made, reasonable access is being given to members of the public. Once the Order has been made it then becomes an offence for anyone to fish for freshwater fish, without a legal right or permission, in the area covered by the Order and the Secretary of State can appoint wardens under section 10 of the Act to see that this part of the Order is complied with.

Wardens are persons who have been nominated for the role by the fishery owners or tenants in the area – a position similar to that of "honorary bailiffs" in England and Wales.

A warden's powers are limited to the right to:

(a) enter onto land to exercise his powers;

(b) ask anyone who is fishing if he has a legal right or permission to do so and if in any doubt may require that person to provide written proof of his entitlement within fourteen days (it should be noted that although fishing without written permission for salmon is an offence under section 1 of the 1951 Act this appears to be the only specific reference to the power for demanding proof of entitlement to fish in the legislation; it is not specifically included in the powers of either fishery board or Secretary of State bailiffs); and

(c) can seize any equipment being used or about to be used if he has reasonable cause to suspect that a person is fishing without legal right or permission or is about to do so.

His powers are restricted to the area covered by the Protection Order and his letter of appointment, which he must produce if required to do so, is his authority to exercise them.

28.7 Powers of arrest

Unlike the position in England and Wales under the 1975 Act a Scottish water bailiff's powers of arrest are not limited to the hours of darkness. Conversely, the provisions of the Police and Criminal Evidence Act 1984, which gives a water bailiff in England and Wales the power of arrest at any time of a person committing or suspected of committing an offence under the 1975 Act, whose identity is in doubt, does not apply.

The power of arrest can only be exercised by fishery board and Secretary of State's water bailiffs – wardens do not have this power.

The offences which an angler could commit (either deliberately or unintentionally) and for which he could be arrested by a water bailiff include:

(a) fishing for salmon without legal right or written permission (section 1, 1951 Act);

(b) fishing for salmon, trout or freshwater fish other than by rod and line (section 2, 1951 Act);

(c) fishing for salmon in the close season (section 15, 1868 Act);

(d) buying, selling or in possession of unclean or unseasonable salmon (section 20, 1868 Act);

(e) buying, selling or in possession of salmon in the close season (section 21, 1868 Act);

(f) taking, destroying, buying or selling juvenile salmon (section 19, 1868 Act); and

(g) possessing unlawfully taken salmon knowing or having reason to suspect that it was illegally taken, killed or landed (section 7, 1951 Act as amended by section 22, 1986 Act).

Corresponding powers are contained in the 1857 Act for offences committed under the Tweed Acts.

TAIL PIECE

This book has tried to explain in simple terms the law relating to fisheries in Great Britain as it affects the angler. Simplification has its drawbacks as it can supply apparently simple answers to complex problems and it is for this reason that I must caution readers not to interpret the contents as supplying a solution, or as applying to any specific situation. In most cases involving the law it is not so much the law itself which is in dispute but the facts, and their interpretation, that are the cause of contention.

This book is certainly not intended to replace professional legal opinion which should always be consulted if a matter is of sufficient seriousness to warrant it.

Part 3

APPENDICES

Appendix A

SOME BASIC HINTS FOR YOUNG (AND NOT SO YOUNG) ANGLERS

(a) Always make certain, if you live in England or Wales, and are old enough to require a licence, that you buy one which covers you for the types of fish you intend to fish for *before* you start to fish.

(b) Always carry your licence with you when fishing and produce it when asked to do so by a bailiff.

(c) Always make certain that you have permission before starting to fish, especially if fishing for salmon in Scotland, by getting permission or buying a day ticket or season permit from the owner or tenant of the fishery or from an approved agent.

(d) Always carry your permit with you when fishing and be prepared to produce it when required to do so by a constable, another angler on the same fishery or a keeper in order to prove your entitlement to fish. If fishing for salmon or sea trout in Scotland it is a legal requirement to produce it to a constable or bailiff.

(e) Know what the minimum size limits are (if any) of the fish you are likely to catch. If you do catch an undersized fish unhook it gently and return it to the water at once with as little injury as possible.

(f) Learn to identify unclean fish and always return, unharmed, any that you catch.

(g) If an undersized or unclean fish is deeply hooked it is better to cut the cast near its mouth and release it rather than risk killing it by trying to remove the hook.

(h) Make certain that you know the dates when the annual close seasons start and finish, on the water you are fishing.

(i) Learn and observe all local bye-laws especially those relating to bait, lead shot and prohibited fishing areas.

(j) Learn and observe any rules that apply to the waters you are fishing - especially if they include the need to move onto another beat at a specified time.

(k) Never be tempted, through frustration or otherwise, to resort to un-ethical or illegal methods to take fish.

(l) Only sell any salmon or sea-trout to a reputable fishmonger, hotel or acquaintance and always produce your licence or permit when you do so.

(m) If you have doubts about a bailiff's or keeper's credentials ask him to produce his warrant or other authority.

(n) Never buy a licence or permit from anyone at the waterside unless he can prove he is authorised to sell it.

(o) Never hand a fish, rod or tackle to anyone who says that he is seizing it unless he can prove he is entitled to do so.

(p) If you still have doubts about a person's powers or credentials volunteer to accompany that person to a local police station to establish his bona fides.

(q) Report any illegal fishing activity to the local bailiff as soon as possible and make a note of the description of the person or persons involved and the number of any vehicle being used.

(r) If guilty of some fishery offence and you are caught by a bailiff or other person in authority do not worsen the position by refusing to cooperate with him.

(s) Report any dead fish or signs of pollution *immediately*.

(t) Do not cross fields containing growing crops - walk around the edge.

(u) Shut all gates after you.

(v) Observe the rest of the Country Code.

(w) Be courteous and considerate at all times to other fishermen.

(x) Remember that angling is a sport to be enjoyed - take advantage of it for that purpose and be content.

Finally,

DO NOT LEAVE DISCARDED TACKLE AND OTHER RUBBISH ON THE BANK - TAKE IT HOME.

Appendix B

SPECIMEN LEASE

AN AGREEMENT made this 16th day of December 1989 between Algernon Septimus Catharsis of Zander Court, Pickerel Street, Roach, and his successors in title, hereafter referred to as the OWNER, and the Big Kipper Angling Club, of 14, Mandalay Way, Britling, hereafter referred to as the TENANT; whereby it is agreed that the OWNER shall lease to the TENANT the fishery known as the Mangoes situated on the right bank of the River Fruit being eight hundred and fifty-five yards in length (the boundaries of which are shown in blue on the attached plan) for a period of seven years commencing on the first day of January 1990 at a rental of £500 (five hundred) per annum, with the option to renew this agreement at the end of seven years for a further period of five years at a rental then to be agreed.

THE OWNER agrees:
1. that the TENANT:-
   a. shall have free access to and from the fishery at all times via routes shown in red on the attached plan and to the area shown in black for the parking of vehicles;
   b. shall exercise the right to fish legally without interruption at all times when legally entitled to do so and to catch and remove such fish as are caught;
   c. may permit other individuals to fish on a daily basis;
   d. may erect one temporary lock-up hut in the parking area, subject to planning requirements;
   e. may, in order to improve the fishery, remove fish by non-angling and control predators, subject to legal authority;
   f. may re-stock the water with the consent of the National Rivers Authority; and
   g. may do such works to, and remove such vegetation from, the banks of the fishery as are necessary to maintain and improve it, and for that purpose take onto the fishery any machinery or vehicle;

2. not to permit any other activity, not connected with the farming of the adjoining land, on the fishery without the previous approval of the TENANT.

THE TENANT agrees:

a. to pay the rent on or before 15 January each year;

b. to pay such rates on the fishery as may be demanded from time to time by the National Rivers Authority and local authority;

c. to indemnify the OWNER against any claim arising from the TENANT'S activities or those of individuals permitted to fish;

d. to occupy the fishery in a reasonable and responsible manner;

e. to avoid damage to crops and disturbance of livestock;

f. to supervise the activities of all using the fishery;

g. to make good, or to compensate the OWNER for, any damage arising from fair wear and tear, such damage to be determined by a joint inspection of the fishery and access routes by the OWNER and TENANT each year before 31 December; and

h. to provide the OWNER annually at the end of the season with details of all fish caught and such other information that he may reasonably require.

Both the OWNER and TENANT agree;

a. that any dispute, or failure to reach agreement as to rent, arising from this lease shall be referred to an independent arbitrator and that his decision shall be binding on both parties; and that any costs incurred shall be borne equally by both parties;

b. to take all reasonable steps to seek legal recompense for disturbance or damage to the fishery arising from pollution or other activity by a third party;

c. that the option to renew this agreement shall be agreed by 30 June 1996; and

d. that this agreement may be terminated by either party by twelve months notice, or by three months notice if the conditions contained herein are not fulfilled by the other party.

Signed:

Witnessed by:

Date:

Signed for and on behalf of the Big Kipper Angling Club:

Witnessed by:

Date:

Appendix C

SUMMARY OF THE SALMON AND FRESHWATER FISHERIES ACT 1975

PART 1
(Prohibition of Certain Modes of Taking or Destroying Fish)

Section 1. Prohibited implements
Section 2. Roe, spawning and unclean fish, etc.
Section 3. Nets
Section 4. Poisonous matter and polluting effluent
Section 5. Prohibition of use of explosives, poisons or electrical devices and of destruction of dams etc.

PART 2
(Obstructions to passage of fish)

Section 6. Fixed engines
Section 7. Fishing weirs
Section 8. Fishing mill dams
Section 9. Duty to make and maintain fish passes
Section 10. Power of water authority to construct and alter fish passes
Section 11. Minister's consents and approvals for fish passes
Section 12. Penalty for injuring or obstructing fish pass or gap
Section 13. Sluices
Section 14. Gratings
Section 15. Power of water authority to use gratings, etc. to limit movement of salmon and trout
Section 16. Boxes and cribs in weirs and dams
Section 17. Restrictions on taking salmon or trout above or below an obstruction or mill race
Section 18. Provisions supplementary to Part 2

PART 3
(Times of fishing, selling and exporting fish)

Section 19. Close seasons and close times

SCHEDULE 1
(Close seasons and close times)

SCHEDULE 2
(Licences)

SCHEDULE 3
(Administration)
Part 1 - Orders
Part 2 - Byelaws
Part 3 - Miscellaneous

SCHEDULE 4
(Offences)
Part 1 - Prosecution and punishment
Part 2 - Procedure

SCHEDULE 5
(Repeals)

(References to water authorities now apply to the N.R.A.)

Appendix D

OFFICES OF THE NATIONAL RIVERS AUTHORITY

Headquarters,
Rivers House,
30-34 Albert Embankment,
London, SE1 7TL
Tel: (071) 820 1603

Anglian Region,
Aqua House,
London Road,
Peterborough,
Cambridgeshire,
PE2 8AG
Tel: (0733) 555667

Northumbrian Region,
Eldon House,
Regent Centre,
Gosforth,
Newcastle upon Tyne,
NE3 3UD
Tel: (091) 213 0266

North West Region,
P.O.Box 12,
New Town House,
Buttermarket Street,
Warrington,
WA1 2QG
Tel: (0925) 53999

Severn Trent Region,
Sapphire East,
550 Streetsbrook Road,
Solihull,
Birmingham,
B91 1QT
Tel: (021) 711 5824

Southern Region,
Guildbourne House,
Chatsworth Road,
Worthing,
West Sussex,
BN11 1LD
Tel: (0903) 205252

South West Region,
Manley House,
Kestrel Way,
Exeter,
Devon,
EX2 7LQ
Tel: (0392) 444000

Thames Region,
Kings Meadow House,
Kings Meadow Road,
Reading,
Berkshire,
RG1 8DQ
Tel: (0734) 593333

Welsh / Cymru Region,
Plas-yr-Afon,
St.Mellons Business Park,
St.Mellons,
Cardiff,
CF3 0EG
Tel: (0222) 770088

Wessex Region,
Bridgwater House,
King Square,
Bridgwater,
Somerset,
TA6 3EA
Tel: (0278) 457333

Yorkshire Region,
21 Park Square South,
Leeds,
West Yorkshire,
LS1 2QG
Tel: (0532) 461889

Other useful addresses

Anglers' Cooperative Association,
Midland Bank Chambers,
Westgate,
Grantham,
Lincolnshire,
NH31 6CE
Tel: (0476) 61008.

Institute of Fisheries
  Management,
"Balmaha",
Coldwells Road,
Holmer,Hereford
Holmer,
Tel: (0437) 276225.

Salmon and Trout Association,
Fishmongers Hall,
London Bridge,
London,
EC4R 9EL
Tel: (071) 283 5838.

British Waterways Board,
Willow Grange,
Church Road,
Watford,
WD1 3QA
Tel: (0923) 226422.

National Federation of Anglers,
Halliday House,
2 Wilson Street,
Derby,
DE1 1PG
Tel: (0332) 362000.

National Anglers Council,
11 Cowgate,
Peterborough
Tel: (0733) 54084.

Ministry of Agric. Fish and Food,
Fisheries Divisions,
Nobel House,
17 Smith Square,
London,
SW1 3HX
Tel: (071) 238 3000.

Department of the Environment,
2 Marsham Street,
Westminster,
London, SW1
Tel: (071) 212 3434.

The Sports Council,
26 Park Crescent,
London,
W1
Tel: (071) 589 3411.

The Countryside Commission,
John Dower House,
Crescent Place,
Cheltenham,
Gloucestershire,
GL50 3RA,
Tel: (0242) 21381.

The Angling Foundation,
23 Brighton Road,
South Croydon,
London,
CR2 6EA
Tel: (081) 681 1242.

The Nature Conservancy Council,
Northminister House,
Peterborough,
PE1 1VA
Tel: (0733) 40345.

The Forestry Commission,
231 Corstrophine Road,
Edinburgh,
EH12 7AT
Tel: (031) 334 0303.

The Royal Society for the
Protection of Birds,
The Lodge,
Sandy,
Beds.
Tel: (0767) 80551.

Appendix E

REGIONS OF THE NATIONAL RIVERS AUTHORITY

Appendix F

SCOTTISH DISTRICT FISHERY BOARDS, CLERKS AND OFFICES

(Shown in clockwise order from the Annan. See also Appendix G)

1	ANNAN	J.E.M.Stevenson Esq, per McJerrow & Stevenson, 55 High Street, Lockerbie.
2	NITH	E.G.Fenwick Esq, per Saint & Co, 26 Castle Street, Dumfries.
3	DEE (Kirkcudbright)	J.W.Campbell Esq, New Cottages, St.Mary's Isle, Kirkcudbright.
4	FLEET (Kirkcudbright)	G.Davies Esq, per McCormick & Nicholson, 66 Victoria Street, Newton Stewart.
5	CREE	G.Davies Esq, per McCormick & Nicholson, 66 Victoria Street, Newton Stewart.
6	BLADENOCH	P.M.Murray Esq, per A.B.& A.Matthews, Bank of Scotland Buildings, Newton Stewart.
7	LUCE	E.A.Fleming-Smith Esq, Stair Estates Office, Rephad, Stanraer.
8	STINCHAR	T.L.Wilson Esq, 1 Church Street, Girvan.
9	GIRVAN	T.L.Wilson Esq, per Murray and Tait, Procurator Fiscals Office, Girvan.
10	DOON	H.S.Campbell Esq, per R.& J.A. MacCallum, 8 Alloway Place, Ayr.
11	AYR	G.Hay Esq, per D.& J. Dunlop, 2 Barns Street, Ayr.
12	EACHAIG	A.T.M.Cairns Esq, Lochloy House, Nairn.
13	AWE	T.C.MacNair Esq, per MacArthur Stewart and Co, Boswell House, Argyll Street, Oban.
14	CRERAN	J.A.M.Smith Esq, per McGrigor & Donald, Pacific House, 70 Wellington Street, Glasgow.
15	LEVEN	J.Sutherland Esq, per McGrigor, Donald & Co, PO Box 13, 224 Ingram Street, Glasgow.
16	LOCHY	MacArthur, Stewart & Co, 87 High Street, Fort William.

17 LOCH SHIEL   E.T.Cameron Kennedy Esq, 95 Bothwell Street, Glasgow.

18 MORAR   M.H.Spence Esq, 8 New Square, Lincoln's Inn, London.

19 LOCH ROAG   G.H.MacDonald Esq, Estate Office, Stornoway Trust, 20 Cromwell Street, Stornoway.

20 CREED   G.H.MacDonald Esq, Estate Office, Stornoway Trust, 20 Cromwell Street, Stornoway.

21 FINCASTLE   A.G.Scherr Esq, Borve Cottage, Isle of Harris.

22 CLAYBURN   A.G.Scherr Esq, Borve Cottage, Isle of Harris.

23 MULLANAGEARAN   D.Shaughnessy Esq, Estate Office, Lochmaddy, North Uist.

24 EWE   Middleton, Ross & Arnot, PO Box 8, Mansefield House, Dingwall.

25 GRUNIARD & LITTLE GRUNIARD   Middleton, Ross & Arnot, PO Box 8, Mansefield House, Dingwall.

26 BROOM   Middleton, Ross & Arnot, PO Box 8, Mansefield House, Dingwall.

27 ULLAPOOL   Middleton, Ross & Arnot, PO Box 8, Mansefield House, Dingwall.

28 LAXFORD   J.D.O.Fulton Esq, per Tods & Murray WS, 66 Queen Street, Edinburgh.

29 INCHARD   N.W.Buchanan Esq, per J.& F.Anderson, 48 Castle Street, Edinburgh.

30 GRUIDE OR DOINARD   W.H.Cormack Esq, per MacKenzie & Cormack, 20 Tower Street, Tain.

31 HOPE AND POLLA   Middleton, Ross & Arnot, PO Box 8, Mansefield House, Dingwall.

32 KINLOCH   A.Sykes Esq, per Brodies WS, 15 Atholl Crescent, Edinburgh.

33 NAVER AND BORGIE   W.McEwan Esq, 105 Culduthel Road, Inverness

34 HALLADALE   Mrs.J.Atkinson, 8 Sinclair Street, Thurso.

35 FORSS   A.T.M.Cairns Esq, Lochloy House, Nairn.

36 THURSO   P.J.W.Blackwood Esq, Estate Office, Thurso East, Thurso.

37 WICK   T.P.Buick Esq, per D.W.Georgeson & Son, 22, Bridge Street, Wick, Caithness.

38 DUNBEATH   Colin Scott Esq, Dunbeath, Caithness.

39 HELMSDALE   J.Douglas-Menzie Esq, Mounteagle, Fearn, Ross-shire.

40 BRORA   J.W.Burrow Esq, Sutherland Estate Office,
                  Golspie, Sutherland.
41 KYLE OF   W.H.Cormack Esq, per MacKenzie &
   SUTHERLAND   Cormack, 20 Tower Street, Tain, Ross-shire.
42 ALNESS   W.H.Cormack Esq, per Mackenzie &
                  Cormack, 20 Tower Street, Tain, Ross-Shire.
43 CONON   Miles Larby Esq, Finlayson Hughes, 45
                  Church Street, Inverness.
44 NESS   J.O.Waddel Esq, per Anderson Shaw &
                  Gilbert, 20 Church Street, Inverness.
45 NAIRN   A.de Candia Esq, Cawdor Estates, Nairn.
46 FINDHORN   W.A.Taylor Esq, per Mackenzie & Grant,
                  Royal Bank Chambers, Forres, Moray.
47 LOSSIE   A.J.McCarten Esq, per Mackenzie & Grant, Royal
                  Bank Chambers, Forres, Moray.
48 SPEY   C.D.R.Whittle Esq, per R.& R.Urquhart, 121
                  High Street, Forres, Moray.
49 DEVERON   Alexander Gibb Esq, 29 Low Street, Banff.
50 YTHAN   Capt. C.A.Farquharson, Estate Office,
                  Mains of Haddo, Haddo House, Aberdeen.
51 DON   G.Alpine Esq, per Paull & Williamson,
                  Investment House, 6 Union Row, Aberdeen.
52 DEE (Aberdeen) J.G.Innes Esq, 7 Golden Square, Aberdeen,
53 NORTH ESK   R.M.Ross Esq, Clydesdale Bank Chambers,
                  112 High Street, Montrose.
54 SOUTH ESK   R.M.Ross Esq, Clydesdale Bank Chambers,
                  112 High Street, Montrose.
55 BERVIE   R.M.Ross Esq, Clydesdale Bank Chambers,
                  112 High Street, Montrose.
56 TAY   R.P.J.Blake Esq, per Condie MacKenzie &
                  Co, 2 Tay Street, Perth.
57 FORTH   H.Robb Esq, 3 Pitt Terrace, Stirling.
58 TWEED   J.H.Leeming Esq, River Tweed
                  Commissioners, Quayside, Berwick on
                  Tweed.

Appendix G

SCOTTISH FISHERY BOARDS

Appendix H

BIBLIOGRAPHY

To appreciate more fully, and to obtain greater details on, some of the subject matter in this book the following publications are recommended as additional reading matter:

Theft Act 1968 (H.M.S.O.)
Control of Pollution Act 1974 (H.M.S.O.)
Salmon and Freshwater Fisheries Act 1975 (H.M.S.O.)
Police and Criminal Evidence Act 1984 (H.M.S.O.)
Salmon Act 1986 (H.M.S.O.)
Stones Justices' Manual, (Annually) (Butterworth & Co, (Publishers) Ltd.) (Shaw & Sons Ltd.)
M. Lloyd Parry, *Fishery Law* (Institute of Fisheries Management, 1976)
Michael Gregory, *Angling and the Law* (Charles Knight,1974)
A. S. Wisdom, *Law of Rivers and Watercourses* (Shaw & Sons, 1979)
W. Howarth, *Freshwater Fishery Law* (Blackstone Press, 1987)
T. W. Beak, *Salmon and Trout Fishing, Law of Scotland* (Gloster Publications, 1955)
The Hon Lord Jauncey, *Fishing in Scotland, Law for the Angler* (W. Green and Son Ltd., 1984)
R. B. Williamson, *Powers of Water Bailiffs and Wardens to Enforce the Salmon and Freshwater Fisheries Acts (of Scotland)* (Department of Agriculture and Fisheries for Scotland, 1985)
Association of Scottish District Salmon Fishery Boards *Salmon Fisheries of Scotland* (Fishing News Books Limited, 1977)

INDEX